# A Taste for
# Trouble

Aniruddha Bahal is the founder and editor-in-chief of Cobrapost.com, an Indian investigative, non-profit website. Previously, he worked for *India Today*, *Down to Earth*, *Financial Express* and *Outlook*, among other publications. He also co-founded Tehelka.com.

Bahal is the author of two novels, *Bunker 13* (2003) and *The Emissary* (2010), and a comic, *The Adventures of Rhea: The Cobrapost Affair* (2015).

# A Taste for Trouble

MEMORIES *from* ANOTHER TIME

# ANIRUDDHA BAHAL

# cntxt

First published in hardback by Context, an imprint of Westland Publications Private Limited, in 2021

Published in paperback by Context, an imprint of Westland Books, a division of Nasadiya Technologies Private Limited, in 2024

No. 269/2B, First Floor, 'Irai Arul', Vimalraj Street, Nethaji Nagar, Alapakkam Main Road, Maduravoyal, Chennai 600095

Westland, the Westland logo, Context and the Context logo are the trademarks of Nasadiya Technologies Private Limited, or its affiliates.

Copyright © Aniruddha Bahal, 2021

Aniruddha Bahal asserts the moral right to be identified as the author of this work.

ISBN: 9789360454623

10 9 8 7 6 5 4 3 2 1

The views and opinions expressed in this work are the author's own and the facts are as reported by him, and the publisher is in no way liable for the same.

All rights reserved

Typeset by Jojy Philip, New Delhi

Printed at Saurabh Printers Pvt. Ltd

No part of this book may be reproduced, or stored in a retrieval system, or transmitted in any form or by any means, electronic, mechanical, photocopying, recording, or otherwise, without express written permission of the publisher.

*To Reema, with love*

# CONTENTS

*Introduction*   xiii

## PART I

| | |
|---|---|
| Beginnings | 3 |
| My Father's Mother | 6 |
| A Memory of Nana-ji | 8 |
| Nana-ji Is No More | 8 |
| Dalda Swimming | 9 |
| Cobra on the Neck | 10 |
| A Meter Reading | 11 |
| Kites | 12 |
| Are Leeches Poisonous? | 12 |
| Bhutan, 1973 | 14 |
| The Loan Shark of Goethals | 15 |
| The List | 16 |
| Feeling Important | 17 |
| 'Can I Have Some Toast?' | 18 |
| Learning Mischief | 19 |
| Tearing Up Letters | 20 |

| | |
|---|---:|
| The Gablu Gang | 21 |
| Playing Badminton | 23 |
| The Tank | 24 |
| The Great Train Robbery | 25 |
| A Bat Called Tony Greig | 27 |
| Awasthi, My Saviour | 27 |
| The Pink Card | 29 |
| The Head Priest | 30 |
| Compass Attack | 31 |
| The Six-pack Tanzanian | 33 |
| Golfing with Nana-ji | 34 |
| Jack-in-the-Box | 35 |
| Gifts from a Genius | 36 |
| Memories of Uncle Jagdish | 36 |
| The Algebra Book | 40 |
| Alexander and Agatha | 42 |
| The Snake | 42 |
| The Famous Polaroid of Bamrauli | 43 |
| Roll Call | 44 |
| Dreams and Nightmares | 45 |
| Smokin' Eyes | 47 |
| Shivaji Sir | 49 |
| The Swimming Gambit | 50 |
| The Spy Who Loved Me | 51 |
| A Love Letter | 52 |
| The Fiancé | 53 |
| Coin in the Bulb | 55 |

| | |
|---|---|
| Running Away | 57 |
| My Neighbours in Bombay | 58 |
| Lingering at the Taj | 59 |
| Meeting Morteza | 60 |
| The Return | 62 |
| Uncle Bharadwaj, the Magician | 63 |
| Canvas Ball Admonitions | 63 |
| The World Record | 64 |
| Sangam, 1984 | 66 |
| The Blessings of Swami Vivekananda | 67 |
| Drills for Indira Gandhi | 68 |
| Yoga Camp, 1984 | 69 |
| The Monk of Benares | 71 |
| A Goat, a Bull, a Buffalo, a Monkey, a Dog, a Cat and a Cow | 71 |
| Niladri Maharaj: Monk, Friend, Counsellor | 72 |
| My First Job | 73 |
| My First Novel | 76 |
| Are You from Allahabad? | 77 |
| Visa Blues | 78 |
| Esha on the Way | 79 |
| Where Is Rhea? | 80 |
| The Video Camera | 81 |

## PART II

| | |
|---|---|
| Starting at *India Today* | 85 |
| My First Byline | 86 |
| Toxic Waste in Delhi | 87 |

| | |
|---|---|
| Night-time Reading | 88 |
| When in Korea... | 89 |
| The Ghost Who Walks | 90 |
| Fare Most Fowl | 91 |
| A New Connection | 93 |
| Night Out | 94 |
| Tsangbosche | 95 |
| The Hound of the Baskervilles | 96 |
| An Alternative | 97 |
| Murder Most Foul | 98 |
| Meeting Omar | 99 |
| Brian Lara's Diatribe | 100 |
| Keeping Wickets | 102 |
| Cooking with Jimmy | 104 |
| Mamu's Idlis | 104 |
| Catching the Big Fish | 105 |
| The Great Game | 107 |
| Indo-Pak Bhai-Bhai | 108 |
| Chai with Justice Chandrachud | 110 |
| Mark Is the Man | 111 |
| Sachin at Twenty-Five | 112 |
| Hide and Seek in Dhaka | 115 |
| Miandad and the Pakistani Dressing Room | 116 |
| Bigger than Bodyline | 117 |
| France, 1998 | 119 |
| The English Pack | 120 |
| Meeting Viv Richards | 121 |

| | |
|---|---|
| Travels with Imran Khan | 123 |
| An Embarrassing Moment | 124 |
| Bets, Lies and Deceit | 126 |
| Lance Klusener Comes to *Outlook* | 129 |
| *Tehelka*: The Business Plan | 130 |
| Board Meetings at *Tehelka* | 133 |
| Fallen Heroes | 136 |
| The Lead-Up To Operation West End | 138 |
| Operation West End: The Goof-Ups | 140 |
| Holi Acrimony | 142 |
| The *Tehelka* Witch-Hunt | 143 |
| The CBI Raid | 147 |
| Up Close and Personal with the Law | 148 |
| The Official Secrets Act | 152 |
| VIP Style | 157 |
| A Live-Streamed Arrest | 160 |
| A Familiar Face | 161 |
| Measuring Corruption | 162 |
| My Bosses | 163 |
| Bunker 13 | 164 |
| Passport Blues | 166 |

## PART III

| | |
|---|---|
| The Birth of Cobrapost | 169 |
| Asha Parekh in Iraq | 170 |
| The Kurdish Disco Dancer | 173 |
| What Did Vajpayee Think? | 174 |
| The Match-Fixing Confessional | 174 |

| | |
|---|---|
| Cash for Questions | 181 |
| Suicide Bombers | 186 |
| The Original Data Story | 187 |
| 'Hello, Welcome, Me the Tony B!' | 187 |
| Diabolical Forensics | 194 |
| Democracy for Sale | 199 |
| Syed's Stories | 201 |
| Washing Dirty Money | 202 |
| The Monster Called Social Media | 206 |
| The Stalkers | 208 |
| The Dirty Eleven | 209 |
| Nero Fiddled, Delhi Burned | 211 |
| A Shaky Aadhar | 213 |
| The Cost of an Exposé | 214 |
| Up in the Air | 215 |
| Operation R: The Assassination Games | 216 |
| Love Jihad Decoded | 219 |
| 'Who Killed Them if They Didn't?' | 221 |
| Breaking the RSS Story | 224 |
| Operation Janmabhoomi | 225 |
| The Hippocratic Oath | 230 |
| Catch Me if You Can | 232 |
| What the Media Wants to Hide from You | 233 |
| The DHFL Scam | 236 |
| Epilogue | 241 |
| *Acknowledgements* | 249 |

# INTRODUCTION

Time, to me, is the interval between two thoughts. When the mind is focused on one thought or altogether empty of thoughts, time ceases to exist. Staying with one thought is what leads us to deep vipasana or meditation. And having no thoughts at all is another form of meditation, a way of vanquishing time itself.

It is in samadhi that we are supposed to reach such a state. That's when, the seers say, the secrets of the world are revealed to us. In the interim, our memories make us who we are, which is why this narration takes the form of memories revisited. Some of my memories, not all. I don't have the courage for that. Some memories are better left in the vaults of the mind.

There are some memories that I savour and relive, not necessarily because they give me pleasure, but because they have been an important part of my journey, and I still wonder how those events even took place. There are some that I keep locked up because unleashing them in public would probably make me even more enemies. If a person can be known by the number of his enemies, then I often think I must be a well-known and well-understood man.

I also have many memories which, if unspooled, would be severely embarrassing. Perhaps they will go to the grave with me.

There are many others that play tricks on the mind. You learn this when you are in court, on the witness stand. And I am sure no journalist in India has been on the witness stand as often and for as long as I have.

Memories rust with the passage of time. I want to write those that I can before they disappear from my grey cells. I want my daughters to know some of them. Perhaps it will give them a better sense of the devils in my head.

My fondest memories are from childhood, which I remember with great warmth. Memories of friends, family, cousins, uncles, aunts and grandparents fill me with nostalgia for those days. Many whom I was close to are no more, and I think about them often. Sometimes I pray for them. Maybe they need our prayers now, more than when they were with us. Who knows?

I also pray that I, and those whom I hold dear, will not lose our memories as we age. I want to be anchored always in the consciousness of who I am and where I am striving to go. I want to be able to be grateful for all the blessings of my life, which for me are tied to the image of Kali. I want my love for the Goddess to only grow.

In the end, we are just visitors on a swirling planet in a vastness that we cannot fathom. Our pursuits are trivial, and as a species, we cannot even seem to work towards our own survival.

# PART I

'I am convinced that most people do not grow up.'

—Maya Angelou

# BEGINNINGS

Family lore and memories on my maternal grandmother's side suggest that we belonged to the 'Khakhar' tribe of the Aryas who inhabited the north-west frontier of India. My mother's late uncle, Shri S.B.L. Kakkar, who was an Indian Administrative Service (IAS) officer, writes in his unpublished autobiography about our ancestors being in the service of the Raja of Ballabhgarh, in modern-day Haryana.

One of our ancestors, he says, came with the raja to Delhi to fight for the Mughal emperor, who had become a symbol of Indian unity against the Europeans. The mutiny, however, collapsed, and my ancestor was arrested, and his execution ordered. His lands in Ballabhgarh were forfeited. But the British, in the larger interests of their empire and fully alive to the hollowness of Indian unity, declared a general clemency, and the Government of India was taken over from the East India Company by the Crown. Writes Kakkar:

> My great-grandfather Ram Chandra was a beneficiary but during this period the family was dislocated and the even tenor of life disturbed. Ram Chandra had served the Mughals in a respectable position and he later became the treasurer of the Raja of Ballabhgarh. He was a rich and powerful man and when the Mutiny of 1857 broke out, he, along with his Raja, joined the

forces of Bahadur Shah, the last Mughal emperor of Delhi. It is clear that he had no great liking for British rule and considered it an act of patriotism to restore the Mughal emperor to his glory in Delhi. Bahadur Shah was taken prisoner by the British and all his allies were in disarray. My great-grandfather was also made a prisoner along with the Raja. His family members ran for safety from Ballabhgarh. Under the clemency of Lord Canning, he was spared his life, but most of his lands were seized by the British Government, leaving him with no means of sustenance. It is also evident that he made peace with the British rulers and one of his grandsons, my grandfather, who was named Faqeer Chand, perhaps because he was born with the blessings of some fakir, was taken into the Indian Railways in a clerical post. It was when he was serving at Etawah, in Uttar Pradesh, that my father was born.

Our ancestor Faqeer Chand was on visiting terms with A.O. Hume, then the collector of Etawah. Hume, apparently, had a great regard for Chand for having brought him in contact with some learned men, chief among them being Khatkhate Baba, a learned Kashmiri who took sanyas after giving up his job as a deputy collector in the service of the British.

My mother's grandmother, Jawahar Devi, belonged to Agra. She came from a family of rich zamindars. The zamindari came to the family while it was in the service of the British Crown. Another tale has it that Jawahar Devi's grandfather was in the clerical service of the collector of Agra. The collector was posted to the Andamans around 1861-1862, and my maternal ancestor readily agreed to go with him. The collector, it appeared, had developed a liking for him for his uprightness and devotion to duty. Kakkar elaborates upon an incident from this time:

> While there, this collector was assaulted by some convicts in the jail while he was making his routine round, and it was my maternal ancestor who took the blow and saved the Englishman.

This Englishman was from the British nobility and allied by relationship to Queen Victoria. My maternal ancestor was shifted for treatment to the European Hospital in Calcutta, and the news of his loyal and selfless service was brought to the notice of the British Government in London. The Queen was also informed, and the British rulers, to show their deep gratitude to the Indian clerk, bestowed on behalf of their Queen a zamindari on him at Agra. They also requested him to ask for more favours, but the only favour he asked was for his son to be made the permanent tehsildar of Agra. The request was no doubt granted and the father of my maternal grandfather lived to be tehsildar for a spell of twenty-five years. He must have done well.

On my father's side, the action shifts to the small village of Bharatganj in Manda, about two hours' drive from Varanasi. My ancestors had built several temples in this village. I make it a point to visit Bharatganj regularly for the love of our ancestral gods. My grandfather's elder brother is quite the standout character of that generation. He didn't take to studies, but he had a nose for business. In the times of scarcity before and during the Second World War, he made a fortune importing corked perfume bottles from Portugal and France. Lore has it that he would have lawyers read to him the acts and conditions governing import and then craft his business strategy accordingly. In those days, banks allowed a credit of forty-five days, and he would spin his investment around three or four times during that period. He became one of the four people in Varanasi who owned a car. His son, Vishwanath Bahal, whom I was very close to as a kid, travelled all over the world for business. He was homeschooled, tutored by Englishmen in English and mathematics. But he didn't inherit the street acumen of his father, and frittered away a large fortune. My paternal grandfather, Vishwambhar Nath, whom I never met, was a school teacher in Handia and Chail, villages now in Uttar Pradesh. It is from him that my father got his hunger for education and for making a life beyond Benares.

Once, in 1985, I accompanied my father's elder brother Bhole Nath to Chail. He was going there for the first time after the 1940s. We took a scooter from the airforce station at Bamrauli and a few hours later, after several enquiries, landed up at a Unani doctor's dispensary. The doctor, hearing of my uncle's odyssey to revisit his childhood home, summoned one of his retired compounders from his house. He immediately recognised my grandfather's name. '*Arrey bahut sajjan aadmi thay, ghantoh padhatey thay. Aur apney taaley se bahut baat kartey thay.*' He was a very civil person. He used to teach for hours. And he used to talk to his lock a lot.

My uncle teared up when he heard that. My grandfather did indeed indulge in a funny superstition that made him talk to the lock on his door, convincing it not to open while he was away!

## MY FATHER'S MOTHER

Tulsi Devi, my grandmother on my paternal side, passed away in 1948, long before I was born. But I have heard my father talk about her. She was from a village near Gaya in Bihar. After her marriage to my grandfather, she never could visit her village again. She was a great devotee of Lord Shiva and walked many kilometres barefoot, every Monday, to visit the Kashi Vishwanath temple. So I have heard my bua say. I often pray for my grandmother, wherever she may be.

A couple of memories stick in my head. Both are sad. One is of my father recalling a time when he was in class eight in a school in Handia, near Allahabad, where my grandfather was a teacher. My father stood first in a contest of some sort and won the princely sum of eight rupees. This was pre-1947. His mother asked him to buy a sari for her, but my father wanted to buy a Sheaffer pen. He had seen a rich boy using one, and dreamt of having his own. Many years later, he often told me that he regretted not getting a chance to look after his mother.

The other story about my grandmother is one I have often heard my bua Rajeshwari Devi tell. Bua was married in her teens in 1945 and moved to Allahabad with her kids a few years later. One day, she decided to go and meet her mother at our ancestral home in Bharatganj. In those days, one would take the train from Allahabad and then, from the station at Manda, hire an ekka to reach Bharatganj.

When my bua reached the ancestral home, she found her mother lying in the courtyard and people standing around her. They were taking her to be cremated. She had died of celebral malaria. It had struck just forty-eight hours earlier, and she was diagnosed too late. It was 1948 and news travelled via telegram. Though my grandmother's sister could make it from Benares, nobody else could. My father was able to reach only after the cremation.

My bua says she was in such shock that the tears only came much later. I cry each time I imagine my bua reaching home that day. I could feel her pain and sorrow when she talked about her mother's death. I was very close to my bua. She was like a second mother to me. Though she passed away a few years ago, she is always in my memories.

# A MEMORY OF NANA-JI

I am less than four years old. It's perhaps 1970. I am with my mother in Meerut, at my grandparents' place near Tilak Bridge.

My Nana watches me play, sitting in the veranda. I am playing with Micky, the family dog. Someone has dropped a bottle on the ground nearby, and glass is strewn all over the place.

'Anu, udhar mat jana,' my grandfather warns me, pointing at the glass.

As I inch closer to the glass, he makes grumbling noises. Then he nearly shouts, 'Nahin.' But I have this compulsive need to gravitate towards the glass. I cut my foot. It's bleeding. My grandmother and mother bandage the wound as my grandfather remains sitting in his chair in the veranda.

He keeps taunting me the whole time, clapping his hands in amusement. 'Achcha hua. Jamai raja toh baat hi nahin sunte hain.'


# NANA-JI IS NO MORE

I have five maternal uncles. My mother is the only sister. Some of my uncles have come to Meerut because Nana-ji is sick. He stays alone in his room. Kids are not allowed inside. Doctors come and go. If I make too much noise while playing, I am immediately rebuked.

One day, Deepak mama gets me an army uniform, complete with a cap and a small toy rifle. I go about creating a racket with it, and suddenly, Deepak mama comes out and breaks it with his hands. When I look back, I realise that everyone was tense because of Nana-ji's ill health.

One day, Nana-ji goes away. His body is placed on a slab of ice. Everybody is crying. Even I know that I have to be quiet. A distant cousin, ten years old, minds me. My mother is all teary, and it makes me cry as well.

All my relatives are crying. Some of them are howling. Everybody walks to the gate of the house in a queue. It's about fifty metres long.

A year later, in 1972, the family gathers again in Meerut. I can feel my grandfather's absence. There are some rare moments of levity, when my uncles come together to scare me. My most sacred possession is my suitcase. It has my toys and clothes, including my precious army uniform. My uncles keep hiding my suitcase and I go nuts trying to find it. I have to keep hiding my things from them. Once, when I think all my toys are lost, I come to my mother and put my head in her lap. That makes Girish mama pull up his brothers. He says I've chosen the safest place to hide my head, and nobody can bully me now.

## DALDA SWIMMING

I've been playing truant. I open the gate of our house and wander right up to the edge of the pond ten metres away—the famous pond in Motijheel, near Nagar Bazar in north Calcutta. The pond, which has no walls around it, hosts a biannual fishing extravaganza. I am four years old, and my Dadu and Didu worry that I'll walk into the pond one day and drown. My mother is even more nervous. So my father decides to teach me to swim.

His palms hold up my tummy while I am supposed to splash around. My father was the vice-captain of the boating team at Benares Hindu University, where he studied for a BSc. He has bulging biceps.

There are some other kids learning to swim in there too. Some are my friends and others not. The show-offs are splashing around in rubber tubes. I don't have one. The next day, my mother fashions me a lifesaver. An empty Dalda tin with a strap looped around it that I can sling around my shoulder. It feels more exotic than a rubber tube, though less convenient.

My father will have none of it, though. He unloops the strap from my shoulder and throws me into the pond. It's only when I gulp and gasp that he considers holding me up by my tummy. I am swimming by the fourth day.

## COBRA ON THE NECK

I am about five. A snake charmer has barged into our house in Motijheel, Calcutta. He is doing his swaying bean show. I am riveted as the cobra sways to and fro. It has many colours and swivels its hood with speed as the bean comes closer.

When the time comes for payment, he quotes a big sum, and my father says, 'Itna thodi hota hai.'

The charmer picks up the cobra and drapes it around my father's neck. The cobra hisses like mad, its hood maybe eight inches from my father's face.

'Shiv-ji ka hai, ashirwad dega,' says the charmer.

I freeze. Montu mama, the landlord's son, runs away upstairs, panicked at the sight.

But my father's composure remains intact. My mother shouts at the charmer. '*Hatao bhai jaldi,*' she tells him.

The cobra stares at my father for a good twenty seconds before the man takes it away.

My father goes up many notches in my eyes after this.

## A METER READING

My father is teaching me how to read the electric meter. 'You should know these things in life,' he says.

We both peer at it. He holds the torch to the numerals. Kilowatts. Watts. And a number that's changing next to a revolving disk. Units.

'Go switch off the sitting-room lights and the fan,' he instructs me. I switch off the lights and the fan in the living room.

'See how the speed of the disk has slowed,' he says. We peer together at the revolving disk. The torchlight darts here and there. I can't make out shit.

'Go switch off all the lights in the house,' my father says. I run off to execute his imperial command. I come back in total darkness. We squint at the meter together. It's still moving, albeit slowly. My father scratches his head. 'The fridge,' he mutters. I go and switch off the fridge. This time, when I look, the disk is no longer revolving.

'So, what are the units now?' he asks me. I focus intently on the disk and mutter some random digits. 'You can't even read right. What's to become of you?' he says.

My mother, who has been watching everything silently, now butts in. 'When your father teaches you, you have to concentrate,' she says.

We have another round of lights being switched on and off. The damn meter reading still remains elusive to me. My father gives up at last. And I've never had to look inside an electric meter again.

## KITES

I am fascinated by kites. I cannot fly them myself, though. I have to depend upon Chhorda in Motijheel. He selects a kite from my collection, ties the knots, and has it in the air in no time. Once a kite is up, he lets me play with the string. I know how to pull to get it to soar like a rocket or dive like an eagle. When Chhorda engages in battle with other kites, he always wins, and I jump around clapping my hands. Their strings cut, the defeated kites descend to the earth erratically, their strings trailing them. There are gangs that roam Motijheel, collecting lost kites like trophies.

## ARE LEECHES POISONOUS?

It is 1973. I am six years old and in the third grade at Goethals Memorial School, Kurseong. It's a boarding school run by the Irish Brothers. Kurseong is near Darjeeling, in upper West Bengal.

My father thinks sending me to a boarding school will make me independent, so he is willing to bear the expense. Nearly half of his meagre salary goes towards sustaining me during my year at Goethals.

There are six playing fields at Goethals. Fields one and two are for the kids in classes eleven and twelve. The hotshot boys, like Allay and J.D. Palden. (I write these names from memory, I don't know if the spellings hold.) Fields three, four and five are progressively shorter and are for the middle school. Field six is right up at the top and for students of classes three and four. It is a small field, 25 x 25 m, and used mainly for football. And everybody wants to be Pelé there.

The field is a good two hundred steps up the side of the infirmary, and the way there is thick with bushes and wet grass. It's also full of leeches.

One day, going up with my friends, I notice that there is blood on my left sock. We are all wearing shorts, and my friends discover six leeches sticking to the sock.

Till then, I have only seen leeches sticking to others. I am terrified of them. Six on my own leg is enough to freak me out. I think I am going to die for sure.

My Naga companions just pluck the leeches from my legs. They enjoy squishing them with their football boots. The blood splatters all over the steps, and they stand, comparing the splatters of the different leeches.

My mind is in turmoil. I am new to Goethals and fairly certain that leeches are poisonous, like snakes, and that even if I don't die immediately, I will in a few days.

One of my classmates from Nagaland further vexes me by shouting, 'The Calcutta boy is going to die.' Then he runs up the steps to the football field.

I want to know when the dreaded hour might arrive and approach a cook with great trepidation. 'I've been bitten by leeches. Will anything happen to me?' I ask him.

'No problem,' he says. He checks both my socks and finds one more and puts some salt over it. It falls to the ground on its own. 'You should carry some salt with you always,' he says, as he packs some for me in a newspaper.

I have rarely been so relieved in my life.

'I won't die from the poison?' I ask him.

He laughs. He holds my shoulders and says, 'No, you won't die. Leeches are not poisonous.'

It becomes a game for me after that, to put salt on the leeches and watch them curl up.

## BHUTAN, 1973

I am six years old and visiting Thimpu with my parents. We are Girish mama and Kamala mami's guests. Girish mama is the financial advisor to the king of Bhutan, and very close to both the king and the crown prince.

My aunt has baked cookies for me. Among the dos and don'ts of the household, I am briefed not to touch the chimney in the card room. It's an open heater, and the iron pipe is always burning hot. In spite of being warned a dozen times, I lose my balance near it and extend my right palm reflexively to balance myself. It burns my palm terribly. I howl like a boy possessed while my mother and aunt minister to my wounds.

The same evening, the crown prince, Jigme Singye Wangchuk, visits mama's house, and I am instructed on how to curtsy and address him if I am at all spoken to.

I have a problem with my pants. They are loose and I don't have a belt. So my mother loops a pyjama string through the loops in my trousers to keep them up.

The whole evening, I sit quietly, bearing the pain in my palm, hoping my pants stay up.

# THE LOAN SHARK OF GOETHALS

At Goethals, we get to bathe just twice a week. That's the time the boilers are heated. The guy who does it is nicknamed 'Paniwala'.

He is a short guy. He always has a filthy black jacket on and has teeth that need brushing. He also always has a whole bunch of boarders surrounding him in a huddle, and I often wonder why. I soon find out.

One day, I see a few friends taking money from Paniwala. He stuffs the currency notes in a matchbox, and when he thinks no one is looking, he gives it to one of the boys.

I think Paniwala is a gentle soul who likes to help boarders. Once the boys get the money (one or two rupees at most), they run to the Blackie brothers, two locals who sell patties and biscuits out of a big trunk they have set up in school.

One day, I hang around while Paniwala undertakes this philanthropic distribution of cash in matchboxes.

I have run out of cash myself. My mother sometimes sends me four or six rupees folded within her letters. I have a field day or two with that, at Blackie's or the tuck shop. But several letters have come and no cash has arrived. I look longingly at Paniwala, hoping that his generosity will extend to me as well.

It happens almost exactly as I hope. Without me asking, he beckons me over and hands me a matchbox. I open it in front of him. Out comes a crumpled two-rupee note. *Jao Blackie jao*,' he says. And I run to Blackie's and gorge myself.

There's no such thing as a free lunch, though. A week later, Paniwala comes to me as I am bathing in the dorm shower and asks me to return his six rupees.

'*Do diya tha,*' I say. You only gave me two.

He scowls at me. 'Six,' he shouts and shows me his fist. I have never seen this side of Paniwala. I am petrified. I don't dare bathe again because I don't want to bump into him. I become constipated as I go to the loo at odd hours just to be sure that Paniwala is not lurking somewhere. I am sure that he is soon going to complain to Sister Anne, and she is going to summon me. All of us are scared of Sister Anne. She is stern and strict and says mean things.

When I see Paniwala from afar, I run the other way. I even write to my parents to send me money quickly so I can solve my stalking problem. Once, Paniwala accosts me in the mess hall. He doesn't say anything. He just gives me a particularly menacing look and goes away. I am getting desperate.

I haven't bathed for a week. The second week, I send a friend to check if Paniwala is near the showers. He reports that he isn't, and I bathe in peace.

Many weeks pass without a glimpse of Paniwala. I overhear a conversation about some parents having complained to Brother Morrow about him. He has been shown the door, no doubt because of his less than legal pecuniary transactions.

I still owe him two rupees, or six, depending on who's counting.

## THE LIST

Winter holidays have started at Goethals, and school is about to close. Parents have been coming and taking their wards away. I am sitting on the parapet at the last turn, waiting for my parents to arrive, but every vehicle pulling up leaves me disappointed.

Maybe I am supposed to stay alone in the dorm during the winter? The prospect is frightening. I ask around. The student population has thinned, but there's a jeep full of students waiting. They are to be taken to Bagdogra airport to catch the flight to Calcutta. I look at them with great envy.

Then somebody starts reading a list of names and finds that one boy is missing. Somebody in the jeep points at me and says I am that boy, and they all yell at me to get into the jeep. But I haven't even packed my suitcase yet. I rush to the dorm and Sister Anne helps me pack. I rush back and everybody curses me, one senior in particular.

But boy, I have never been happier to have my name on a list.

## FEELING IMPORTANT

That guy who shouted at me particularly harshly from the jeep? Well, we do eventually get even.

When we get on the flight from Bagdogra to Calcutta, the air hostess comes looking for me. She has a piece of paper with my name on it, and keeps asking the boys where I am, till the guy who shouted at me points her my way.

In our school, if anybody comes looking for you with your name on a chit, you are probably in trouble. The boy has a big smirk on his face. I am just about shitting my pants again. What have I done wrong this time?

But the air hostess smiles at me and says that the captain has called me to the cockpit! My father is an aerodrome officer at Calcutta airport and is pally with the Indian Airlines pilots. He's told one of his pilot friends to invite me to the cockpit.

I walk the aisle like a champion with my Goethals mates looking on in awe. I spend ten minutes at the front of the Caravelle plane. The pilot tells me to fetch a friend if I would like to, so I go back like a hero and pick up the guy who is sitting next to the guy who shouted at me.

Everyone watches as I heroically escort my Goethals senior to the cockpit. He is so overawed, he doesn't say a word, even as the captain asks me about school and explains this and that in response to my silly questions.

When we get off at Calcutta, everybody looks at me in a different light. And when I return to school after the winter break, I find that my reputation at Goethals has amplified to stratospheric levels. I am the guy who got called to the cockpit.

The seniors stay off my back.

## 'CAN I HAVE SOME TOAST?'

I have just returned home after one year of boarding school. I am seven years old. When I was admitted to Goethals, my parents made me skip class two. I jumped straight from class one at Auxilium Convent in Calcutta to class three in Goethals.

After one year there, I join St Mary's in Dum Dum. A year away from home has possibly ironed out my brattishness, at least for a while. My mother says I've become very well mannered at home.

At Goethals, toast was a luxury. If we were lucky, we could sneak out of the dining hall during breakfast and throw slices of bread into the tandoor to crisp them up. It all depended on the mood of the cook, and whether there were senior boys ahead in the queue. They usually shooed us juniors away.

One day, I ask my mother, 'May I have some toast?'

'Sure,' she says and goes about her chores.

After a while, I ask her again, and she looks at me and says, 'Oh, you mean right now? Why didn't you say so?'

I get my toast. A few weeks later, I return to my brash and bratty ways. My mother remarks on it for a long time. She says, 'I liked that Goethals made you polite, but now it's all gone.'

## LEARNING MISCHIEF

The first books I read are by Enid Blyton. *The Famous Five* and *The Secret Seven* series. And *The Naughtiest Girl in School*.

As a seven-year-old, I am profoundly taken with the mischievous antics of Elizabeth Allen. My life revolves around the moment when the clock strikes 4 p.m. My mother won't let me go out and meet my buddies before that. We have a bunch of things to do—roam the streets, play football or tennis-ball cricket with bricks for stumps. Or 'I spy'. Or generally make mischief.

My brothers-in-arms are up and about at 3 p.m., and I can hear them making a racket. The hour I have to wait before joining them is pure suffering. I ritually ask my mother every ten minutes whether I can go. She looks at the watch and says, 'No, it's not four yet.' That hour is her siesta time, and she hates it when I jump around creating a disturbance and poking her in the back to ask questions.

I suffer for many days. Then a bright idea comes to me, possibly from one of Elizabeth's antics. I figure out how to jump the clock by one hour. I poke her in the back and when she lazily asks what the time is, I say it's four, and off I go like a rocket.

Four is also the time she gets up to make tea for herself. It goes on like that for a few days till somebody comes by and watches are compared. My mother looks at me and asks, '*Tumne kuch kiya hai?*' You have done something, haven't you? And my impish smile gives me away.

My father bans Enid Blyton for a few days. 'Those books give you all the wrong ideas,' he says.

## TEARING UP LETTERS

The Motijheel post office stands in a lane adjoining the pond. My mother deposits twenty rupees every month in a postal account in my name. I think she did that till I turned eighteen.

Right in front of the post office, hanging from a telephone pole, is a post box. On most days, it's full to the brim, with letters sticking out of its mouth.

One day, Atom and I find ourselves in the lane, and I notice the post box. A few letters are sticking out of it. I go up and pull them out. It must be close to the new year, for the bunch includes greeting cards. Atom and I look at them and then throw them in the drain.

We return again a few days later and do the same thing. This time, we tear up the letters and dump them in the drain. I don't know what kind of sadistic pleasure we get out of it. I often think of what we did then, and cringe.

I come back again a few days later and look around and push my hand into the post box. I bring out a whole bunch of letters and tear them up and throw them in the drain. This time, I feel a hand on my neck and someone wallops me.

'*Ki korchish tui?*' says the man. What do you think you are up to?

I keep silent. He starts picking up the pieces from the drain. Other people gather around him, wanting to know why he is so agitated. While they are talking to each other, I take off like the wind and don't stop till I am in the safety of my home.

Of course, I cannot tell anyone what Atom and I have been up to. For several days, I don't venture out for fear that I'll bump into the guy who walloped me. Maybe he is worried that I have torn up one of his letters, which could explain him sifting through the torn pieces in the drain.

Then, one day, the man walks right past me. He doesn't recognise me. I feel a flood of relief. A week later, I notice that they have installed a different post box at the same place. It is a tall one, fixed to the ground. You can't put your hand in and pull out letters.

All these years later, apologies to those unknown people whose letters we tore up.

## THE GABLU GANG

Atom is irritated with me. '*Tui ki korchilish? Atto deri kano?*' he asks. What the hell took you so long? His voice is cracking and his eyes are agitated. We have some pressing business. The Gablu Gang is down on the street, and we are busy knotting water balloons to chuck at them from the roof. Atom snatches a balloon from my hands. His fingers are more dexterous. He knots like a sailor. I grab the efficiently knotted balloon back from him, look over the ledge, and smash it down three stories at the Gablu Gang.

*Puch.* It hits Gablu smack in the face. I duck down.

'*Ki holo?*' asks Atom. What happened?

'*Gablur mathar taakey giye laglo*,' I answer. Hit Gablu right in the middle of his bald spot.

Atom replays the scene in his mind and doubles up with helpless laughter. He is afraid he'll be identified as the culprit, so he doesn't glance over the ledge. He knots another balloon and hands it to me. I peer down cautiously. We are on someone else's roof. Atom's neighbour's, to be precise. The old couple who live here haven't seen us sneaking up. The old man is quite scary when he waves his cane around like a hockey stick. It took a lot of persuasion by Atom to get me to follow him up to the roof.

I unleash the second balloon, and it catches Tukun on his arm.

'Who is doing this?' shouts Gablu. His gang is getting hammered. They too have balloons at the ready, but the enemy can't be seen.

I lurk behind the ledge. If they see us, they can (and will) come and complain to the couple about the illegal operation underway on their roof. That will have undesirable consequences. But Atom grows bolder. He too wants to sling down a few from the roof. He gets up slowly and peeks over. The Gablu Gang, instead of scooting, is sticking around, trying to solve the mystery of the Holi ambush.

Atom swings his arm wildly, nearly clipping my ear.

'*Ki korchish?*' I snap. What the heck are you up to?

He swings laboriously and lets fly in the general direction of the Gablu Gang. We hear the dull thwack of a balloon hitting human flesh.

'Who is doing this?' We hear Tukun bark.

Atom is too impatient not to sneak a look over the ledge, even as I try to hold him back. He is spotted.

'*Oidike dyakh! Atom achhey*,' shouts Tukun. It's Atom!

'*Aami boleychhilam dekhish na*,' I whisper fiercely at Atom. I told you not to look, asshole.

Atom is brimming with nervous laughter. He is hugely satisfied with himself, for Gablu is massaging his cheek, where the balloon must have hit him.

Once he has recovered, Gablu rattles the gate of the house. He rings the bell. The old man berates him. '*Kano ghanti press korchhish? Electricity bill ta tui dish naki?*' he snaps. Are you going to pay the electricity bill you're racking up by pressing so hard?

'Atom is throwing balloons from your roof,' Gablu complains.

The gang begins to climb up, with the old man leading the way. Atom nearly pisses his pants. 'Now what?' he asks.

I motion for him to jump to the next roof. There's a two-foot gap. Atom's face goes white. 'Do it quickly!' I tell him, hoping he'll go first.

'You first,' he says.

The old man is about to step onto the roof. I make a running start and jump. It's easy. I hide behind a water tank on the next roof. Atom is scared, and the Gablu Gang and the old man are already there. '*Atom ki gandogol korchish tui? Aiekhane kano?*' Atom, what are you up to? What are you doing up here?

The Gablu Gang has assembled behind the old man. As the old man shakes his head, Gablu lands a kick on Atom.

'He kicked me!' Atom complains to the old man.

'No more balloons for you,' says the old man. 'I'm going to tell your mother how naughty you are.' He seizes Atom by the ear. The gang pounce on our balloons and replenish their arsenal.

## PLAYING BADMINTON

A memory from when I was about eight years old. Ramanath is about twelve. We play badminton with Raju standing as a net in the middle. He wants to play as well, but we take turns trying to hit him with the shuttlecock. Raju keeps running after the shuttlecock, and we keep pushing him away. To make himself useful, he collects the shuttlecock from the ground each time it falls, but we still don't let him play. This goes on for a few days till he comes with his mother one evening, and we have to change our ways.

# THE TANK

It is 1974. Anita masi has come back from London for a brief while. She is the daughter of Dadu and Didu, our landlords. But they are more like family. She took care of me when I was a baby. Soon after marriage, Anita masi (I call her Ta, the last syllable of Anita, as I couldn't pronounce her name) moved to London with her husband.

Montu mama, her youngest brother, has primed me with the news that Ta has brought a toy tank for me. I am super excited. He tells me that it can shoot. I can barely sleep that night. A tank that can fire is the dream of every kid.

I think Ta is hesitant to give it to me because Tutul is present. Tutul is Anjali masi's son and Ta's nephew. He is also my buddy, as is his sister Munmun.

The next day, when Tutul isn't around, Ta gives me the tank. It is awesome! A good eight inches in length and four inches high, and battery powered. Montu mama explains the controls to me. And then he lets it rip. It has a rolled-up fire cracker inside and a hammer that falls on the reel, making a blasting sound with smoke accompanying it. Munmun flees to the other room as soon as the tank starts firing.

Tutul hears tales about the tank from Munmun and comes home at once to see it. He is jealous that Ta has given it to me and not to him.

The tank is one of my go-to toys when I have to impress my friends. Once, in Allahabad, a friend shows me a tank he has received as a present. Bobby shows it to me like it is the coolest thing he has ever seen. He doesn't even let me touch it! It is only about four inches in length. I tell him that I have one about three times bigger. He doesn't believe me and mocks me heartily.

A whole bunch of them end up coming to my house to see my answer to Bobby. His tank is just a model. They don't believe that mine can run on its own steam and fire.

I still remember Bobby's face when my Sherman tank gets rolling. His mouth opens and it doesn't close.

## THE GREAT TRAIN ROBBERY

I am eight years old. My mother and I are travelling by the Kalka Mail from Calcutta to Delhi. We are going to attend my uncle Deepak's wedding in Meerut.

My father saw us off at Calcutta. Our luggage fit into a single large leather suitcase. It's black in colour, and my father has pushed it underneath the side berth opposite our cubicle. By the time we got on the train, the floor of our cabin was full, so the suitcase had to go outside.

My mother's eyes stray to the suitcase while talking to me. My father had told me to take care of my mother and not give her trouble.

An affable gentleman chats us up. He is wearing a blue nightsuit. We unpack our bedding on our berths. Or my mother does, I daresay. We are travelling with our bedding rolled up in green canvas cloth, with leather straps to hold it all in. I fall asleep rather quickly. At some point, if I remember right, the noise of the moving train wakes me up, and I find my mother awake too. She smiles at me and gives me some water to drink. The affable gentleman is sleeping soundly, or at least pretending to. He doesn't have any luggage.

Just before dawn, I wake up to my mother's voice. She is agitated. Our suitcase is missing. The ticket collector comes. People from other berths join in the search for the suitcase. I am fully alert now. I look around for the gentleman in the blue night-suit. He is no longer on his berth or anywhere else.

My mother is really disturbed. 'It's only a suitcase. We'll get many more,' I say. But she is inconsolable.

In those days, suitcases didn't have wheels. Well-meaning co-passengers take a description of the suitcase from my mother, and go to neighbouring coaches to hunt for it. In my zeal, I walk around with some of them, crossing several coaches. The junction between coaches in those days was very shaky and sometimes without side-rails for adequate protection.

I overhear one passenger remark to another, 'What kind of mother is she? She is letting her child cross bogies. She has only been robbed of her suitcase. Somebody might now rob her of the kid.' I scowl at him.

Nothing comes of our search. My mother regrets the one moment she drowsed off. She was awake almost all night. The ticket collector and others suspect the man in the blue night-suit. He must have waited till my mother fell asleep and walked off with the luggage.

'There's a big gang operating on this route,' the TT explains. 'They reserve berths like normal passengers and look around for anyone who is travelling to attend a wedding. Because they know that there's a chance there's jewellery in their luggage,' he says.

My uncle Deepak comes to receive us in Delhi. My mother cries. A lot of her own wedding jewellery was in the suitcase. My mother is very sad. Strangely, she remembers that in the middle of all this, I asked her whether my studying hard would make her happy.

## A BAT CALLED TONY GREIG

The whole family gathers together in Meerut for a week for my uncle Deepak's wedding. The uncles and nephews play cricket all day. I am eight years old and the permanent fielder. My cousins humour me by letting me bat first, but my turn lasts all of one ball. For hours after that, I run around fetching the ball.

We have a new parchment bat from a local shop. It has Tony Greig's name emblazoned in red at the top. Meerut has always been the sports-goods capital of the country. I am glum because my cousins always trick me and I don't get to handle the bat much. My cousin Madhav takes pity on me and says that I can bat till I get out six times. I get out six times in about ten deliveries and field for four hours after that.

The silver lining is that I get to take the bat home. It survives fifteen years, though the handle frays in the later stages of its life.

## AWASTHI, MY SAVIOUR

I am in class five. It's 1975, and I am new in town. I have just moved to Allahabad from Calcutta and am going to St Joseph's College. A new school. No friends. I have been dubbed

'Army launda' for the time being as I come from Bamrauli, where the Central Air Force Command is stationed. My father is not in the Indian Air Force. He is a senior aerodrome officer, training air traffic controllers. But such subtleties fail to register with my classmates.

I am new meat. Up for assessment. I have joined the class a few months into the year, after various alliances and cliques have already been established. Vibhor and Sanjay and Kapoor have been cornering me after class. They have been coming at me with hostile intent for two days in a row. Both times, I have just about managed to wriggle away and run towards my bus stop and the safety of senior students.

On the third day, they corner me by the stairs. There is no way to evade them. It's also a matter of pride. They have challenged the upstart army launda to a fight. Three to one. For all my false bravado, I am scared. Things get hairy. Some pushing and shoving is initiated, and I am mostly at the receiving end.

That's when Awasthi comes by. He is tall for our class and muscular, and nobody messes with him. I know him, but he isn't my friend or anything.

'*Kya hai, kya bakaiti chal rahi hai?*' (Hey, what's this bullying going on?) he asks with the swagger that only a boy confident of his hell-giving abilities can muster.

'*Yeh army launda hai,*' says Kapoor by way of explanation, but more like an insult. '*Apne ko samajhta hai,*' he adds. He's an army kid. Thinks no end of himself.

'*Hum army laundey nahin hain. Bamrauli mein rahtey hain par air force ke nahin hain,*' I say meekly. Not like the said army launda at all.

'*Toh army launda bhi hua toh kya? Bakaiti kaahey ko,*' says Awasthi. So what if he is an army boy, why bully him? '*Chalo nikal lo yahan se nahin toh hum abhi jhapiya dete tum sab ko,*' he threatens. Get lost or I'll slap you all.

The equation changes. They stand down, not knowing how to factor Awasthi into the mix. Awasthi walks me to the bus stand. We strike up a friendship. Awasthi now practises law at the Allahabad High Court.

# THE PINK CARD

Mrs Jacobs is our class-teacher in class five. She is a disciplinarian. She wants pin-drop silence in the classroom when she walks in. She has already warned me a few times. It isn't even my fault. I sit surrounded by Kapoor, Vibhor and a few others who go haha heehee continuously over their infernal jokes. They also throw chalk and pinch neighbours for no reason.

I have defended myself vigorously against Kapoor's pinches, much to his surprise. And have even pinched him back. He is not pleased. He is itching to get back at me for this insolence.

Mrs Jacobs comes in suddenly. She catches Kapoor yakking away at me. He has actually been threatening me about what he will do to me after school.

Mrs Jacobs gestures to him. 'Get up, Kapoor. Come here and kneel against the wall,' she says. This is standard practice in school. The lowest punishment threshold.

Kapoor goes on a bizarre accusation spree. 'I wasn't talking, miss. Bahal was calling you names. I was only defending you,' he says.

I look at him, aghast.

'What was he saying?' asks Mrs Jacobs.

'He was saying that you are very ugly and that's why you shout at us,' says Kapoor, out of the blue.

The ground moves beneath my feet. I go numb with fear.

Mrs Jacobs goes red. She glares at me. 'Did he?' she asks in general.

Vibhor gets up and says, 'Yes, teacher.'

'No, teacher, I didn't say that at all,' I say vigorously. I'm almost trembling.

'I know how to handle you,' she says ominously. She turns away and begins the day's lesson.

I sit through the class with mounting dread. When she walks away at the end of it, I think that's the end of the matter. But no.

A boy from another class comes running up. 'Who is Bahal? Father has called him to his office,' he shouts with great glee.

'*Lagi teri aaj,*' says Khanduja. You are well and truly screwed.

He is the first friend I have made in school.

Ours is a Catholic school. Convents, as they are called. I forget the name of the Father who was junior school headmaster then. He looks at me over his spectacles. 'Take this pink card and get it signed by your parents. One more of this and you will be expelled,' says Father.

Pink has never been my favourite colour.

## THE HEAD PRIEST

As a kid, my bua takes me to the Kalyani Devi temple near Attarsuiya in Allahabad. She is deeply religious and attends Hanuman kathas twice a week. I often tag along.

The head priest at the Kalyani Devi temple is an elderly person. He is thin and short, and likes interacting with kids. He always has the same question for us. Coming up close, his eyes intent on my face, he asks if I am studying in an English-medium school. I say yes. Then he leans in further and asks, '*Fir batao, what maney kya?*'

'Kya' is the literal translation of 'what' in Hindi. So, essentially, the question is also an answer. You can read it as 'What means what?' But it can go without the question mark too, as an answer.

As a kid, I think this is the height of cleverness. Many years later, when I visit the temple, the priest doesn't recognise me at first. But when I ask him, '*What maney kya*', he smiles in recognition.

## COMPASS ATTACK

I am in class six at St Joseph's College, Allahabad. Our class-teacher, Mrs Moore, has taken a shine to me. I have the onerous responsibility of locking and unlocking the classroom for the quarterly tests. This has bestowed upon me an exalted status, which some of my classmates resent.

It has also perhaps made me a little self-important. I have been throwing my weight around and threatening to report miscreants who don't leave the class soon enough after the morning test is over. I've needled many classmates, and there are clusters of dissent where my domineering stance is being discussed.

Dinkar, our resident maths prodigy, has been tattled on once too often. A few weeks ago, he had to bear the brunt of a Mrs Moore offensive, and his emotions swing from resentment to anger to fear to vengeance. His desk is in front of mine and some guys are having a go at him because he is easily provoked and jumpy.

Khanduja throws a chalk at him while Mr Tripathi takes the Hindi class. Dinkar's neck swings back and forth as he tries to identify the culprit. Sitting right behind me, Khanduja takes aim with his middle finger and snaps another piece of chalk at the back of Dinkar's head. The chalk bounces back and settles on my desk.

Dinkar swings around with unusual intent. He eyes the piece of chalk on my desk, and his cortex processes it as evidence. He turns back and starts fiddling with his pencil box. I think he too is hunting for a piece of chalk to snap back at me. But he swivels around and before I know it, stabs a compass at my chest and swivels back with such speed that Mr Tripathi doesn't realise anything is amiss.

Nobody else knows what has happened. I unbutton my shirt, pull my singlet down and look at the bloody puncture. Dinkar swings around and looks at it. He is scared now, and apologetic.

'Sorry, sorry,' he whispers pleadingly.

The others have caught on by now. They are egging me on to rat on him to Mr Tripathi, whose favourite phrase happens to be '*Murga bun*'. This consists of either squatting on the floor with your hands coming up from under your legs and your fingers holding your ears or standing with your knees bent at right angles and back pressed to the wall. It's a painful posture that you can't hold for long. But the moment your body droops, Mr Tripathi is on you like a hound, whacking you on the back with cupped hands.

But for some reason, I say nothing.

I still have the scar from the compass attack. Years later, when Dinkar is posted at the Indian embassy in Colombo, I remind him of the incident, and we laugh about it.

# THE SIX-PACK TANZANIAN

The Civil Aviation Training Centre, where my father was posted, received several trainees from different countries in Africa for communication and air traffic controller courses. There were also ground training courses for pilots.

Songoi was a strapping specimen of a man from Tanzania. I don't remember which course he had come for, but I have two enduring memories of him. One, he could take a blow to his abdomen like it was nothing at all. Two, he was an expert diver—all symmetry, and even flipping somersaults from the diving platform at the swimming pool. We kids used to watch him with our mouths open.

He would flex his abdominal muscles and invite us to have a go with our fists. The kids would line up ten deep, each one believing it would be their fist that would make Songoi bend over with pain. But he never even flinched. A relay of us would come at him, but still his belly remained taut like rawhide.

Once, Debashish, a senior student in our colony, taunted Songoi. 'They are only kids. You want to appear superior to kids? They have no strength,' he told him.

We all looked at Songoi. Would there be a fight?

Songoi was calm. 'You can also try, my friend. Let's see how much power you have in your fist,' he said.

'You will get hurt,' said Debashish.

'Are you backing off? Are you afraid of African power?' asked Songoi. He lifted up his T-shirt, tightened his abdomen muscles and told Debashish to have a go.

Debashish couldn't back off now. He swung his arms in preparation, flexed his muscles and did some loosening up. Songoi watched him with a poker face. We kids looked at each other. Somebody said, '*Aaj toh Songoi khatam.*' Somebody else said, '*Aaj toh Debashish-da ka haath toota.*'

Debashish took a wild swing. Songoi didn't flinch. He had muscles of steel.

'That was girl power, my friend. Girl power,' he said, pulling down his T-shirt and walking away. Debashish blushed.

## GOLFING WITH NANA-JI

I tag along with my mother's maternal uncle, a former IAS officer, when he goes golfing in Meerut. My aunts and others discourage me as they are concerned about whether I will be able to walk for so long on the greens, being only ten years of age. But I insist. For a while, they pack a three-legged foldable stool for every trip so that I can sit on it on the fairway. But I don't see anyone else sitting and feel embarrassed to be the only one. So I never take it out of the car, though Nana-ji always asks.

I can never understand who is winning. Just that the game involves a bunch of grown-ups hitting a white ball with some swing and punch. The first day, I go running to the ball and retrieve it for the guy who has hit it. The men tolerate it a few times. Then they start to admonish me. I cannot understand why they are getting mad at me for providing this voluntary service. Nana-ji defends me against them. '*Arre doita hai. Meena ka bachcha hai,*' he explains. Some of them apparently know my mother.

Quietly, when no is looking, he comes up to me and says, '*Anu, ball mat uthaya karo. Wahin rehne doh.*' Don't pick up the ball. Let it be.

I don't pick up the ball after that. But the reason for their annoyance puzzles me for a long time.

## JACK-IN-THE-BOX

At a family gathering in Delhi, my cousin Madhav hands me a box, saying he is unable to open it. I try my luck. It seems easy. The top turns and I unscrew the lid. As it comes off, out shoots the scariest jack-in-the-box. It looks like a cobra. Throwing the box away, I jump back a few feet. Everybody bursts into laughter.

I bring that box home to Allahabad. I think I have more fun with it than any other toy I own. I try the box on my friends, my father's colleagues, my teachers and a whole bunch of strangers. There are generally two kinds of reactions. People are alarmed and drop the box or are hypnotised by fear.

I try it on our English teacher, Mrs Gandhi. She is frightened and turns red, but doesn't say a word. Later, she tells other teachers in the staffroom how she controlled her panic in front of the students.

Once, I take out the cobra and the spring and rig them up in the sugar box my mother dips into for her afternoon tea. Her afternoon routine is like clockwork. At four o'clock, I listen from the next room, waiting for her outburst. She screams, and I get a shouting.

Some months later, I loan the box to a naval officer who is attending a PGT course. He wants to take it home to scare his nephew and promises to bring it back within ten days. With a great sense of misgiving, I hand it to him. He never brings it back. I have never been so disappointed at the loss of a toy.

## GIFTS FROM A GENIUS

It is 1978. I am eleven years old. The extended family has gathered at Girish uncle's place in Delhi for two weeks. My eldest maternal uncle is visiting from the US. He is the celebrated physics professor Dr Jagdish Mehra. His life's work is contained in the many volumes of *The Historical Development of Quantum Theory*.

He had left India in the 1950s on a Max Planck scholarship and worked on his PhD under Werner Heisenberg and Wolfgang Pauli. He is known to have paid his way through university by coaching science students who were his seniors.

For us cousins, he is a mythical genius. He has brought presents for all his nephews and nieces. I get a Casio calculator. It's a decent-sized one, and considerably valuable as gifts go. Back in Allahabad, it becomes my prized possession and lasts me till college.

Girish uncle's house is on Humayun Road. All of us cousins jump the wall and go to Khan Market to play video games. It costs only a rupee for about two minutes.

Once, we are all walking in Khan Market when Jagdish uncle asks each one of us what we want for a gift. My cousin Ashish goes for cricket stumps. Cousin Chayan asks for batting gloves. I choose wicket-keeping gloves. They last me till university!

## MEMORIES OF UNCLE JAGDISH

My first memories of my uncle Jagdish are from 1972, when I was five years old. It had been a year since my maternal grandfather passed away. I used to call Jagdish uncle 'Bade mama' as he was the eldest of my uncles, and he used to call me 'Jamai babu'. Of course, at the age of five, I had no idea of his accomplishments. On his visits to us between 1978 and 1991, he spent a lot of time in the evenings regaling us with stories, and so did Girish mama. Some of these stories stayed with me.

In 1952, while on a short teaching assignment at Dayal Singh College in Delhi, Jagdish uncle befriended Vice President Sarvepalli Radhakrishnan. He became very fond of my uncle, and admired his deep knowledge of literature and history, besides his first love—physics. He called my uncle 'Jagdishan', and insisted that he visit him at least once a week.

Around this time, my uncle Girish had become a lecturer in history at Meerut College. One day, he received an aerogramme addressed to Jagdish Mehra. The sender's name was Albert Einstein.

He rushed to Delhi with the letter, and Jagdish uncle opened it. It read:

Dear sir,
Apart from the unwarranted praise I find your characterization of my convictions and personal traits quite veracious and showing psychological understanding.
  With kind greetings and wishes
  Sincerely yours, Albert Einstein.

It happened like this. Jagdish uncle had written a prize-winning essay titled 'Albert Einstein's Philosophy of Science and Life'. He had given a copy of the essay to Paul Arthur Schilpp, the editor of *Albert Einstein: Philosopher Scientist*, when Schilpp visited Allahabad University, and he passed it on to Einstein. This episode further inspired Jagdish uncle to go abroad for further studies.

And that's when fate intervened. Georg Leszczynski, a German journalist and a friend of my uncle, had been trying unsuccessfully to get an audience with the vice president. Uncle Jagdish arranged it in no time. Leszczynski then introduced my uncle to the German ambassador, Dr Alfred Meyer. The ambassador was impressed and arranged for him to get the Oskar Henschel Fellowship for Advanced Studies.

With all his varied interests, Jagdish uncle wanted to be a writer, and wrote a letter to his hero, the poet Aldous Huxley, asking for guidance. Huxley replied: 'You have the best of themes. You have studied quantum theory, which is the greatest revolution in human thought. Most of its creators are still alive; work with them and learn from them how this great field developed in the twentieth century and write about it. Go and work with Pauli in Zurich.'

Radhakrishnan also wrote a letter of commendation to Bertrand Russell for my uncle, and arranged a fellowship for him at Trinity College, Cambridge, to work with Paul A.M. Dirac.

Jagdish uncle arranged passage for Rs 1,400 from Bombay to Zurich via Aden, Port Said, Cairo, Alexandria, Athens and Genoa. He set sail on the SS *Australia* on 1 October 1952. My mother, then ten years old, remembers his departure from Meerut. Girish mama went to Bombay to see his elder brother off, and was inconsolable on the train ride back to Meerut. He cried all the way. His companion-in-arms had gone away.

In Zurich, the famous physicist Wolfgang Pauli invited my uncle to work with him, but also suggested that he meet Werner Heisenberg in Gottingen, for Heisenberg was one of the pioneers of quantum mechanics. Jagdish uncle followed his advice and met Heisenberg at the Max Planck Institute in Gottingen. Heisenberg took him under his wing, and every Wednesday, Jagdish uncle would have lunch at the physicist's home. On these visits, Heisenberg advised all his children to speak in English and eat vegetarian food as a courtesy to my uncle. After lunch, the two proceeded to Heisenberg's study, where my uncle would record their conversations and interviews. Heisenberg also introduced him to several other notables, including Max Born, Eugene Wigner and Sin-Itiro Tomonaga. In the spring of 2001, my uncle finally completed his life's work: *The Historical Development of Quantum Theory*.

In the 1950s, Jagdish uncle went to the UK to interview for a position in the Department of Scientific and Industrial Research. Lord C.P. Snow interviewed him as chairman of the committee. At some point, Snow asked him about his most memorable moment since his arrival in the UK. Apparently, without a hint of a pause, my uncle replied, 'When I gave my shoes to be shined by an Englishman.' In spite of this remark, he was selected, and Lord Snow became his lifelong friend and admirer.

The other memorable account was of Jagdish uncle's first meeting with Paul Dirac. In his own words:

> My first meeting with Paul Dirac took place in Cambridge in 1955. I had just returned to England after a couple of years with Heisenberg in Gottingen. A historian friend of mine in Cambridge, knowing of my great hero worship for Dirac, offered to take me with him to St John's College to dine at the High Table. He thought we might see Dirac there. I went with him and true to his word, he showed me that Professor Dirac was sitting there. We sat down. The weather outside was very bad, and since in England it is always quite respectable to start a conversation with the weather, I said to Dirac, 'It is very windy, professor.' He said nothing at all, and a few seconds later he got up and left. I was mortified, as I thought that I had somehow offended him. He went to the door, opened it, looked out, came back, sat down, and said 'Yes'. In April 1970 when I reminded him of this, he reflected and said: 'Mehra, I wonder why I did that, because I must have already known that the weather was windy when you said it, unless it had changed since I went inside.'

Besides Jagdish uncle's much-quoted work on the historical development of quantum theory, he published close to 225 papers and essays in various scientific journals. He also wrote biographies of Richard Feynman (*The Beat of a Different Drum*) and Julian Schwinger (*Climbing the Mountain*).

Many physicists remember him for a symposium titled 'The Physicist's Conception of Nature', which he organised in 1972, on the occasion of Dirac's seventieth birthday. Uncle got all the speakers to sign the dinner menu. He passed that on to his brother Girish. As kids, we used to pore over the names.

Jagdish uncle's interests extended far beyond science. He conducted interviews with T.S. Eliot, Aldous Huxley, Louis Aragon, Carl Gustav Jung and Jean Paul Sartre. The Jagdish Mehra Collection at Houston University has been praised by UNESCO as 'absolutely unique as a scientific and cultural source'.

This, then, was my magnificent uncle. Hearing the tales about him as kids, my cousins and I would feel hugely inspired. Two of my cousins ended up pursuing doctorates in the US after graduating from IIT Kanpur in the 1980s.

## THE ALGEBRA BOOK

One evening in 1978, when I am in class eight, I discover that my algebra textbook is nowhere to be found. Our maths teacher can sometimes get nasty, and he always checks to see whether we have our textbooks on our desks.

In the evening, I go to borrow one from Pinto, whose elder brother Bobby has a spare and is willing to give it away. Pinto tells me he will bring it for me in the morning.

In the bus the next morning, I discover that Pinto has given the book to Rishi, another friend. He is a year junior to me, but uses the same textbook.

I panic and tell Pinto to tell Rishi to give it to me, because it was promised to me first. But Pinto shrugs me off. It's none of his concern, he says. He tells me to deal with Rishi myself. I turn to Rishi and ask him politely, but he tells me to buzz off. Then I pull his school tie and rough him up and snatch the algebra book.

Rishi is quiet the rest of the way to school. Once we reach, he goes and complains to Mr Moore, who is his class-teacher. Mr Moore is another unpredictable piece of work. He can be nasty or amenable to reason, depending solely upon his mood.

Two kids come up to me before the morning assembly, saying that Mr Moore wants to have a chat with me. Something about me snatching some algebra book. I nearly shit my pants. He has sent two louts who must have made nice careers later in the collection business. When I set off to meet him, they stop me and say that I need to take my algebra book along. Once I have it, they snatch the book from my hands and frogmarch me like a felon to Mr Moore.

'Is this the guy?' Mr Moore asks Rishi. He nods his head. Mr Moore doesn't even ask me for an explanation. He tells me he will announce my 'crime' in the assembly, and I will have to come to the mike and apologise in front of the whole school.

The two goons let me go and laugh all the way to their desks.

I rush to my class-teacher, Mrs Bannerjee. She is married to a colonel in the army and new to our school. I request her to speak to Mr Moore and sort out the issue. It will be so embarrassing to be called up in front of the school assembly, I plead with her.

'How dare he do that!' says Mrs Bannerjee, and walks off to confront the principal. From a distance, I watch the two of them in deep confabulation, trying to infer the outcome.

She comes back and tells me she has fixed the problem. 'He won't do any such thing to a student of mine. And I hope you will behave yourself in future,' she says. I nod my head vigorously. I have never been so relieved about anything.

Mrs Bannerjee doesn't stay long at St Joseph's College. Her husband gets posted out. But I always remember her fondly for that one incident.

## ALEXANDER AND AGATHA

I am in class eight, and I am a bookworm. I can devour a book a day. I am hungry to read even during the lunch break. The library is in the hall in front of the principal's office, and Miss Pereira is the school librarian. I befriend Miss Pereira and she lets me sit in the library behind closed doors. In a month, I finish six Agatha Christies and reread many of Alexander Dumas's books, even though I only get to read during the forty-five-minute lunch break. I try to get my friend Sameer Sah into the game, but he gets bored of it in three days and goes back to lunch. There is only so much reading some can stomach.

## THE SNAKE

Our school bus, a Bedford truck with seats, lets us off at the last stop in Bamrauli. I am walking home. For the past few days, I have been playing a game. I look ahead, then close my eyes and see if I can maintain a straight line for the next thirty metres. I open my eyes when I get to a turn in the road, and repeat the process.

As I near home on the last stretch with my eyes closed, I hear a sinister hiss. I open my eyes in dread. A cobra lies curled on the path with its hood raised. I stare at it from a safe distance. It lowers its hood and slithers away. I run to my mother in excitement, shouting that I have just escaped certain death!

## THE FAMOUS POLAROID OF BAMRAULI

My father goes to the US for three months' training in 1979. He brings back a remote-controlled car for his niece's daughter and a Polaroid camera for the house.

Before the car moves on, I play with it a few times, but always under the supervision of my father. The packaging says it has to be kept 'dust-free', so my father has the floor mopped about five times before handing me the remote to fiddle around with. The car never can move in a straight line and often strays into un-mopped territory. Then I get a tongue-lashing, and there has to be some more mopping.

The instant pictures from our Polaroid camera become all the rage in Bamrauli. People land up unannounced, all dressed up, and demand to be clicked. Even our dhobi hears of this magic device that shits out pictures in a minute, and asks to be shot.

Taking a picture is a ritual in itself. The brochure says the subject should stand between three and four feet from the camera. My father calls for an inch-tape and has the distance measured so nothing can go wrong with the shoot. Film is costly and not available in India. One has to depend on relatives flying in from somewhere abroad.

After a lot of measuring, the picture is taken. The film that emerges is flapped around. I still don't know what that was for, but my father said that's what the shopkeeper had told him to do. I would wave the snap maniacally and see the images come to life. We would all be awestruck by the phenomenon.

## ROLL CALL

Rajesh sits next to me in class ten. He lives in mortal fear of his teachers, which makes him obnoxious and irritating. He is the kind of boy who always does his homework and always brings his textbooks to class.

He is also rather selfish with his stationery box. We sit three to a row in class. His roll call comes at eleven and mine at five.

One day, I get it into my head to prank him while Mr Pradhan, our class-teacher, is taking the morning's roll call. He gets very irritated if a student doesn't respond immediately. The expected responses are either 'Yes, sir' or 'Present, sir'.

As soon as my name is called and I have responded, I start muttering under my breath with great anxiety, '*Yaar ab kya hoga, chemistry ki kitab toh mein laana hi bhool gaya.*' I forgot my chemistry books, now what?

'What chemistry?' says Rajesh. 'There's no chemistry class today!'

'*Bhaang pi hai tumne? Aaj PT break ki jagah chemistry hai. Abhi kitab nahin laya toh Jhingur pel dega,*' I say. Have you eaten bhaang? We have chemistry after the PT break. If you don't have the book, Jhingur will lay into you.

We call our chemistry teacher 'Jhingur'. The nickname is from before our time and just rolled on.

Rajesh gets so riled at my bit of disinformation that he completely forgets his roll number. Then Pradhan lights into him for a good minute or so.

'Class mein sona mana hai. Raat mein soye nahin thhey kya,' Pradhan lambasts him. It's forbidden to sleep in class. Didn't you sleep at night?

Rajesh stands up, says 'Sorry, sir', and sits down sheepishly.

The next day, I distract him with something else. Once, I make a terrible face and say to him, 'Don't fart, okay. If you want to fart, go to another desk.'

'I didn't fart,' says Rajesh.

He is so upset that he misses Pradhan calling his roll number thrice, and the teacher has to throw a piece of chalk at him to get his attention.

The joke catches on, and students in the row ahead of us start winking and colluding with me. But Rajesh never gets the game. He once asks me seriously why, in my opinion, he never hears Pradhan call his roll number. I look straight at him and tell him to get his ears checked. 'Sometimes a lot of wax closes up the ear drums,' I say sombrely.

## DREAMS AND NIGHTMARES

I am in the ninth grade, and the quarterly term exams are on. I am having bad dreams about physics. A whole bunch of my friends are underprepared. In fact, I doubt any of us has even opened the textbook. The bloody thing is a nightmare. Vernier calipers, vectors, oscillations, simple harmonic motions and god knows what else. For all I care, they can all go and drown themselves in some black hole.

'What a wonderful idea it would be if they postponed the dates for a bit,' says Vikram Singh.

'Yes,' says Henry Dutt. Bajpai is more colourful. '*Saala padre karega nahin jab tak koi issue na ho jaye,*' says he.

'*Woh kyun karega bey? Dates fix hain,*' I say. The Fathers aren't about to change exam dates on a mere whim.

But in the dead of the night, I chew on an idea. After the departure of Father Patro, Father D'Souza is a new and benign presence. Father Patro was beloved of the students, but rubbed the teaching staff the wrong way with his strict rules. They had connived to have him sent packing after a food poisoning incident among the boarders, which led to the boarding school being shut down.

Henry is getting desperate. 'If I fail, my father is going to whip me,' he says.

'*Thoda aur padhne ko mil jayega agar date aage ho jaye,*' murmurs Vikram.

That night, I have another dream. I am staring at my physics paper like an idiot. All the other students are writing away furiously as I nibble on the top of my pen. I wake up in a sweat and decide to do something about it.

First, I undertake a recce. I watch Father D'Souza at his routine. The time he comes to work. The time he is alone in his office. The time he takes to pray in the chapel.

My school bus arrives one hour before school starts. I have developed a certain conviviality with the office peon, and while he does his morning dusting, he allows me to practise typing on a typewriter. I use the phone there to call the padre in his office.

'Father D'Souza, this is Fuste calling from the Indian Certificate Secondary Examination board offices in Delhi,' I say in a grave baritone.

'Yes,' says Father.

'We need to postpone the start of the internal quarterly exams in October. I believe your quarterlies are starting from 15 October. We need the dates shifted by two weeks,' I say.

'That can be done,' says Father D'Souza. 'It's in our control.'

'Please issue the circular. It's mandatory for all schools,' I say.

'Yes, Mr Fuste,' says Father obligingly.

Next day, at assembly, I make a prophecy to Ashish Chopra, the school captain. 'I have a feeling the quarterly exams are going to be postponed,' I inform him with an air of clairvoyance.

'Can't be. I overheard a meeting in the staff room. The question papers have gone for printing. They were worried that they wouldn't come in time for 15 October,' Chopra says.

'I just feel it, Ashish,' I say, trying to sound deep. 'I had a dream.'

'Balls to your dream,' says Chopra.

On the stage, Father D'Souza gets up during the assembly and announces that quarterly exams have been postponed by two weeks.

Chopra looks at me with his mouth open.

'Did you have something to do with this?' he asks suspiciously.

I do have a bad reputation.

## SMOKIN' EYES

I have a great physics teacher in class nine. His name is Joe Shankar, and he is an Anglo-Indian. He stays in the teachers' quarters close to the school. He conducts private tuitions there after school and sometimes chats with us boys as we wait for our bus.

Inside the classroom, he has a habit of walking around with a cane, and if you cannot answer one of his questions or aren't paying attention, he asks you to hold your palm out and strikes it with his cane. He drinks too much and smokes even more. His skin is a deathly yellow. His liver seems to have all but packed up.

He calls me one day and asks me in front of a group of senior boys, 'Have you seen somebody blow smoke from their eyes?'

The boys smile. 'Yes, you have to show him, sir. These guys think it's not possible,' says one boy.

'It's a very special talent. Only he knows how to do it in all of Allahabad. They say there are two guys in Delhi who can do it, but I haven't seen them,' says another boy as he nudges me.

I am all set for the show to begin. We circle Mr Shankar, and my eyes are glued to his eyes. He blows out a few puffs of smoke normally through his mouth and then nods his head and gets close.

My eyes have gone dry. I am hardly blinking. I am watching his eyes with as much concentration as I can muster.

I feel something hot touch my thigh. I jump back.

'Wow, did you see that?' says a senior.

'Wow, that was great,' says another.

'Did you see that?' one of the boys asks me, smiling.

'No,' I say.

'How could you? You were jumping around so much,' he says.

'Okay, I'll do it again,' says Shankar. 'This time, watch closely, because I won't repeat it a third time, and you will never get to see someone blow smoke through their eyes.'

We huddle up again, and this time my concentration is even greater.

This time, too, as I stare mightily into Joe Shankar's eyes, I feel something hot on my leg and jump back. They all squeal with laughter and that is when I realise that the joke is on me.

Later, every once in a while, I would bring an unsuspecting boy to witness the smoke coming out of Joe Shankar's eyes and watch him jump back as Shankar touches his thigh with his lighted cigarette.

Shankar would always say, 'The only guy who fell for it twice was Bahal here.'

Joe Shankar died of a diseased liver in the early 1980s. I still have memories of him walking around in the classroom with a cane in his left hand while jiggling a piece of chalk in his right hand.

## SHIVAJI SIR

Shivaji sir is correcting trigonometry exercises. Exercise 10A. Two students in the rows in front of me have forgotten to bring their homework notebooks. *Slam!* One of them covers his cheeks and ducks down to provide our maths teacher with as little space as possible to manoeuvre his landing. The other trembles in horrific apprehension of what is coming. *Slam!* The second boy hits the wall from the force of the slap. Sir leaves them abruptly. No words spoken. Nothing like a little physical exercise to get the blood circulating.

Elsewhere in the classroom, a flutter of surreptitious activity is underway. Notebooks are being exchanged and answers are being copied at great speed. Speed is the only antidote to pain. Shivaji sir looms over my desk menacingly. He flips the pages of my notebook. He sees that I have not only completed exercise 10A but gone ahead and completed 10B and 10C as well. He looks at me approvingly and walks on. After that day, he never again checks my maths homework. And I never do it.

# THE SWIMMING GAMBIT

It is time for the 200 m swimming relay. Four guys, 50 m for each. That's two lengths. I am in class ten and in Gold House. Bunny D'Cruz has been looking for swimmers for his team. Somebody hears me spout a few tall ones about my swimming capabilities. And Bunny D'Cruz has taken note. He calls me over. 'I hear you can swim well,' he snarls, almost like an accusation. Since there are twenty other people around, I say, 'Yes, teacher.'

The next thing I know, I am in the Gold House relay team. A replacement for one of their star swimmers.

I am a good swimmer with a steady, slow pace. I have been doing fifty lengths every day at the swimming pool in Bamrauli. And it's a good 40 m pool. But I have no technique to my strokes. No science behind my swimming. And hardly any speed.

I have never been in a swimming race, and here I am in the relay finals. An anchor at that. I watch the three guys go before me and I am swinging my arms and behaving like a big bad dude. Doing all these warm-ups but nervous as hell.

We are leading by nearly half a length, and I can hear D'Cruz going, 'We have it, we have it. Bahal is going to ace it. He is going to kill them.' He is also making faces at the Green House master, Mr Wilson. My turn comes to dive into the water, and I go at it any which way, my arms and legs swinging wildly.

By the end of one length, all four of us are abreast. I have lost the lead. D'Cruz is running along the side of the pool, waving his hands and egging me on. He is panicking. I can see him from the corner of my eye as I gasp for breath. A win would give Gold House four points.

I am soon passed by all the houses, and I no longer hear D'Cruz's voice. By the time I reach the end, the other three boys are already out of the water.

I get out of the water and feign a limp, as if I have had a sudden cramp.

All through that year, whenever D'Cruz sees me, he starts flapping his arms, imitating my strokes!

## THE SPY WHO LOVED ME

I am in class ten. There is a surge of conjunctivitis at school. It's the weather, perhaps. Students in all the classes are developing a glaring redness in their eyes. Their eyes start watering. And then they leave school for home.

I am in the throes of teenage rebellion. And Tighmanshu Dhulia is my partner in crime. We want to see *The Spy Who Loved Me*.

He doesn't have the nerve to go at first. I have rubbed my eyes over and over again. They are not very red, but red enough. I haven't been able to make them water, though. I shine up my face with some saliva.

I go up to my class-teacher with a kerchief over my eyes. She doesn't even ask. Just gestures for me to leave with a wave of her hand. I go down and wait for Tighmanshu. He copies my antics and soon we reach Palace Theatre in Civil Lines and watch our first Bond film.

After that, we bunk school regularly.

# A LOVE LETTER

Meena has fascinated me for some time. She is my friend Jay's sister. She is in class ten and I am in class nine. The journey to school binds us every morning and afternoon. For weeks and months, I have nursed my crush. I plan to give her a love letter on the bus. I work on it for many days. I write about her eyes, her looks, and the way she carries herself. I pinch lines from a birthday card. 'You cannot smell a rose without a part of the rose remaining within you.'

I choose the novel *The Good Earth* by Pearl S. Buck. At night, I cover it with a thick piece of brown paper and insert my letter between the cover and the title page of the book. Meena usually sits with a gaggle of nosey girls inside the bus, and I don't want my letter to fall out of the book and be seen by them.

The next afternoon, I pounce at a moment when the nosey girls are preoccupied with a game of clap-and-song. I hand the book to Meena gingerly and motion to her that there is something inside the cover. She starts to open the book and then Susan, one of the nosey girls, jumps on it. 'Let's see, let's see,' she squawks. As her hands fumble with the book, the cover comes off and the envelope with the letter spills to the floor.

My heart leaps into my mouth. Susan leaves the book for Meena. She is clawing at the envelope now. She takes out the four sheets of paper and starts reading. I shrink lower and lower in my seat. Susan reads my letter aloud in the bus for all to hear. Meena snatches a sheet or two back. By this time, the nosey girls are having a relay match with the sheets, handing them around like batons. There is a brief moment when Meena manages a furtive glance at me, and I see how horribly embarrassed she is.

The sheets reach Jay and as he reads them, his face turns crimson, though it's hard to say whether it's with anger or shame. I bend my eyes to my textbook as if chemistry engrosses me more than anything else in the world.

## THE FIANCÉ

Meena rings me at home. 'You are so stupid. Why did you have to keep the letter inside the cover? Couldn't you just have kept it in the book? My fiancé wants to meet you now.'

'Your fiancé?' I blabber.

'Yes. He meets me every Thursday when my mother's around. Come to our house in the evening,' says Meena and hangs up.

'Fuck,' I say to myself.

Sanjay has heard of my situation. He is in a class senior to me. 'Randhir is a black belt,' he informs me with relish. I swallow; my throat is suddenly dry.

'Can you come with me to Jay's place?' I ask Sanjay.

'Why would I come? Her father's an air commodore. Mine is just a wing commander,' replies Sanjay.

'What's that got to do with anything?' I ask.

'Take Ravinder. He's planning to join the army. If a fight starts, who's going to help you?'

'A fight?' I gulp.

'Why do you think they've called you?' he points out. 'Can you fight?'

'No,' I say.

'Then take Ravinder,' advises Sanjay again.

Ravinder ponders over my problem. He is due to join the army on a short-term commission. 'I can teach you some moves,' he says.

'No, no. I want you to come with me, please. If you come, her fiancé won't do anything,' I plead.

Ravinder eyes his own biceps. He stretches his limbs. 'I can't. I have some other stuff to do,' he says.

'Bhai, come on,' I urge. 'You remember Suman? She wants to meet you at my house,' I add. A few days earlier, he had told me to take a love letter to Suman, a girl who lives in our colony. She had torn up the letter in my presence and told me to tell Ravinder to go to hell.

'Really?' asks Ravinder.

'Yes,' I say, lying through my teeth.

'But you told me that she tore up my letter,' he says.

'She did. That was to make you suffer. She wants to meet you now. I'll arrange an afternoon of chess at my place. You can give her lessons,' I say.

Ravinder's eyes light up. He agrees. In the evening, both of us land up at Meena's place. The dog barks on seeing us.

'Who's he?' asks Meena.

Ravinder stands outside the gate and out of earshot. His hands are on his hips.

'My brother,' I say.

'Since when do you have a brother?'

I ignore her question.

'Didn't you like my letter?' I ask.

'You are an idiot! Why did you have to give the letter to me in the bus, in front of everybody?' Meena asks.

'I gave you a book, not a letter. That girl Susan! I could kill her,' I defend myself.

'You should have kept the letter inside the book and not inside the cover,' says Meena conspiratorially.

'Why didn't you snatch the letter from Susan?' I ask.

'How could I? It was all over the place, and I didn't know what it was. You know, you are stupid. I had to pass the letter on to my fiancé. He is upset,' says Meena.

'Fiancé! You are just in class eleven!'

'But our parents have matched us up. Randhir is a black belt. He has a business. He is the son of the CNC,' says Meena.

'CNC?'

'The air marshal. Let me go call him,' says Meena. She goes inside.

Meanwhile, Ravinder is getting agitated, standing at the gate. He doesn't know what the hell is going on. He keeps gesturing at me to move my ass and leave. He starts walking away.

I panic. I do not fancy meeting Randhir by myself.

Meena comes back. 'I've got to leave,' I say. 'My brother's leaving for Delhi. He's due to catch a flight to Honolulu.'

'Honolulu?' asks Meena, her eyebrows arched.

I am already outside the gate and walking away. I am barely a hundred metres out when Randhir comes along. He looks like a big, strong guy. He starts hollering and waving his arms for me to come back. But I have caught up with Ravinder and both of us scoot the hell out of there.

## COIN IN THE BULB

I am in class ten and suffering from a bout of adolescent angst. Rebellion; a scattered mind. Studying is for idiots, that kind of thing. Textbooks put me off. But my mother is on to me. With love. With threats.

I toy with the idea of short-circuiting the electric supply of our house. No lights and utter darkness: the perfect excuse to not study.

I put a twenty-five paisa coin at the base of a bulb and screw it into the holder. Then I switch on the bulb. It makes a crackling noise and the lights go off. The CPWD electricians are called. This is the home of the principal of the Civil Aviation Training Centre, and people come when they are called.

Every time the electricians mend the fuse and switch on the mains, the lights go pop. They are in a fix. There are two different phases in the house. As soon as they tie the wire up on a fuse (there's no Havell available in 1981), I tiptoe into a bedroom, unscrew a bulb from its holder, insert the coin and re-screw the bulb. When the electricians switch on the mains, boom goes the bulb. They rush to that room to see what has happened.

The only snag is that every time they go into the room, I have to quickly retrieve my coin for fear of being caught. By this time, the junior engineer, Mr Bora, has arrived. He and his team put their heads together to understand the phenomenon, like detectives faced with a particularly inscrutable crime. One of them opines that the entire wiring of the house has to be changed. But Mr Bora is a tenacious man.

By this time, I have managed to procure my mother's permission to go to Dolly's place to study. But as I leave, the lights come back on and I have to repeat my prank, lest I be found out and pronounced guilty once everything starts working in my absence.

One of the electricians finds my movements within the house terribly suspicious. He reckons that bad things happen in rooms I have just been to. I overhear him telling his colleague, '*Bhaiya jiss kamre se nikalte hain wahan ka fuse udta hai.*' Whichever room he steps out of, the light fuses there.

He comes and tells me to stand next to him as he fixes the fuse. I have no problem doing that, as I have already coined up another bulb. He scratches his head when it fuses again. As the game progresses, Mr Bora too begins to harbour suspicions about me. Indeed, my reputation in Bamrauli is not enviable. Any mischief anywhere and I am bound to be on the list of suspects by default.

Still, they can't figure out what I am doing to unleash this electrical anarchy. As I come back once again from coining up a holder, Bora sends me out of the house and locks the door. Smart engineer. He goes about unscrewing all the bulbs in all the rooms. When they discover the coin, the household erupts.

I am confronted by my father and Mr Bora. I have to muster up all my skills at pretending innocence to say, 'How the hell do I know how that coin got up there?'

## RUNNING AWAY

My mind is running wild. I am in class ten, preparing for the ICSE board examinations, but I don't want to study. One evening, in late December, I run away from home in Allahabad. I take about three thousand rupees from my parents' safe and catch the bus to Rewa, where, as a fifteen-year-old, I talk my way into a government guest house at 2 a.m.

In the morning, I make my way to Satna, and from there, take a train to Bombay. I have never been to the big city before.

I believe my English-speaking skills will get me a job, and I will earn enough to buy a motorbike. I badly want one. My parents have refused to get me one because it's not safe, they say. I have no intention of returning for a few years. I just don't want to study.

# MY NEIGHBOURS IN BOMBAY

I reach Bombay in the afternoon and take up residency in a dormitory over a shop near Victoria Terminus. The rent is something like twenty rupees for a night. I stay for three, sleeping next to a salesman from the shop below.

Some rooms in front of the dorm have been let out. Every night, a man brings up the same hooker, and after their business is over and he goes to sleep, she comes out of the room and chats with us in the dorm. I am fascinated by her.

There is another guy in the dorm, a Bihari traveller, who gets it going with her in the kitchen. There is no one there at night, and they shut the door, but not all the way. I can hear a continuous shuffle on the floor or the counter and her occasional exhortations for him to finish quickly before the other guy wakes up.

Once, while this is happening, the guy does wake up and comes out of the room to look for his partner. He taps me on the shoulder and wakes me up to ask if I have seen her.

'Who?' I ask.

'*Arre usko!*' he says. Her.

I feign ignorance. He is a big, burly man, and I don't want him to think I'm a friend of the Bihari. He hears shuffling from the kitchen and heads there. But before he can enter, the woman comes out.

'*Kya kar rahi hai? Kya kar rahi hai?*' he asks.

'*Arre chai rakhi hai janu,*' she says. Making some tea, darling.

That pacifies him, and he goes back to his room.

She winks at me.

# LINGERING AT THE TAJ

I have heard of the Taj Mahal Hotel at the Gateway of India, and I intend to go there to look for a job.

I am travelling around in black-and-yellow Fiats. The taxis are cheap. Around six rupees for a ride of two or three kilometres. I am extra careful. I keep my money inside my socks. Paying the fare means a whole ritual of pulling my socks off and peeling two-rupee notes from one of the bundles I have sneaked out of my parents' safe. The taxi drivers watch me with incredulity.

I land up in the lobby of the Taj and hang around. Sometimes on this sofa, sometimes on that. Sometimes near the pillar. Sometimes sauntering around. I search for somebody who looks important and can perhaps give me a job.

I identify a tall person. To me, he looks like the kind of person everybody listens to. For over half an hour, I try to muster the courage to talk to him, but somehow can't bring myself to do it.

I decide to take a walk on the seafront and if the person is still around in the lobby when I return, I will talk to him. On the waterfront, I see many Arab Sheikhs walking around with their burqa-clad wives. In those days, Bombay still scored over Dubai.

When I go back, the guy is still there. He is tall, with wavy hair, is wearing a white suit with a blue tie, and has hair coming out of his nose.

I walk straight towards him.

'Excuse me, I would like a word with you,' I say.

I am nearly as tall as he is. He is taken aback, and stops whatever he's doing to listen to what I have to say. 'Yes?' he asks.

'I am looking for a job, and I wonder if you might be able to help,' I say.

He sizes me up with disdain. I cannot make out if he is a fair Indian or a foreigner.

'I am sorry, I would be the wrong person for that,' he says. 'Go ask them.' He waves at the Taj lobby staff.

I smile at him and slither away, feeling like kicking myself. My paper-card dream has fallen apart.

## MEETING MORTEZA

After the humiliation in the Taj lobby, I roam the waterfront, then sit on the parapet, contemplating the future. What am I to do? I have run away from home. Where should I go to try for a job next? My stolen money is going to run out in a few weeks.

Two Iranians are chatting with each other next to me. One has two fingers missing on his left hand. To put things in context, it is 1981 and the Iraq–Iran war is raging. Though I can't understand all that they say, I can vaguely tell that they are talking about friends who went to war and are now no more.

The Iranians have a conscription system going, to feed the front lines. I try to butt into the conversation now and then as a convivial neighbour sitting on the parapet next to them.

'Khomeini is no good. He is bad for Iran,' I say.

The Iranian with the missing fingers gives me a thumbs-up with the hand that is missing fingers. The other one is silent. He has a beard. He eyes me each time I speak.

'It is true. See what I lost! I lost many friends. We run away from war,' says the missing-fingers guy, waving his hand again.

They keep chatting in Persian, and after some more banalities, the missing-fingers guy leaves. The beard sits on. I introduce myself. He says that his name is Morteza, and he is studying in Bombay—I forget what. He is staying as a paying guest in Colaba. Then he scolds me.

'You cannot talk about Khomeini in the open like this. We all know he is not good, but we can't talk about it or we are khalaas,' he says.

He then starts probing. Where am I from? What am I doing in Bombay? The usual stuff. And all of a sudden, I feel like confiding in him. I tell him how I have come to Bombay to get a job so I can earn enough money to buy a bike.

He starts counselling me.

'Look at me and my friend. Our families are in Tehran. We want nothing more than to be with our families over New Year, which is a few days away. And look at you here: you have left your family. There is nothing more important than family,' he says.

Then he tells me that I should call my family; they must be worried. In those days, there were no STD booths. You could only book long-distance calls through the telephone exchange.

Morteza takes me to the telephone exchange. It's a good ten-minute walk or more. He books a call on my behalf to Allahabad. There are different gradations of call costs—normal, urgent and lightning. There are brokers who, for the cost of a normal call, will facilitate a lightning call.

My mother comes on the line. She is distraught. I tell her I will be back in two days. I am in tears.

# THE RETURN

I get into a general compartment of an express train the next day, after buying a ticket to Allahabad. I find standing space next to the loo. Somebody sits on top of my suitcase.

I am squeezed in next to a person from Madhya Pradesh. We spend twenty hours standing, then sitting, next to the toilet. People climb all over us every five minutes to pee.

I tell my story to the guy, and he listens with great empathy. Then it's his turn to confide in me. He has just been released on bail after three years in prison. He doesn't tell me for what. He is now trying to piece his life together.

After twenty hours, as people reach their destinations, there's just enough space for one person to be able to squat with his back to a partition. It's the MP guy's turn to have that space. But he offers me the spot. I fall asleep after a long time.

When I wake up, we are almost in Allahabad. My cousin Rajeev is waiting for me at the station. I see him on the platform from afar, but am not ready to face him. Instead, I climb down to the tracks on the other side of the platform, cross over, and exit the station.

When I reach home, I open the outer gate quietly. We live in a big bungalow—government accommodation. I don't have the courage to knock. I go to the window of my parents' bedroom and peep inside. My mother is lying on the bed, her arm covering her face. My father and his sister are having a conversation about me. My cousin has apparently called to say that I haven't come on the train.

I knock on the door.

# UNCLE BHARADWAJ, THE MAGICIAN

We called him Laloo uncle. He was a classmate of one of my uncles, and an amateur magician. At Deepak mama's wedding, he made my cousin Madhav disappear using a canvas bag. He could make pencils feel like rubber sticks, and he even had a plastic replica of human poop, on which he would place my grandmother's house keys, to her great agitation.

Many years later, he taught me how to disappear a thimble from one's forefinger and pull it out of someone's nose or ear. I became very adept at it, and still try it on kids, to their great astonishment.

It was always a pleasure to meet Laloo uncle. He never lost pace, even with several stents packed into his heart. And he always had to entertain everyone with card tricks.

I was very fond of him because he landed up at home in Bamrauli in 1981, the day after I returned from Bombay. He sensed the tense atmosphere and took me out to play cricket on the lawn. We had good fun for many hours. He never advised me. Never rebuked me.

I got a message from him on 28 November 2019. It read: 'Dear friends, I left for my heavenly abode yesterday at 1545 hrs. My earthly take off is at Dhruv Ghat Mathura at 1100 hrs. Subsequent programme will be intimated later. God bless you all.'

# CANVAS BALL ADMONITIONS

My father's way of disciplining me was often to narrate tales from his growing-up years and juxtapose them with my 'privileged' upbringing. I will leave you with some of his one-liners. They need no explanations.

'I never knew what breakfast was till I got married,' he would say.

'When I was ten, I visited Allahabad from Handia with my father. Every day, I would ask my father to get me a ball. I wanted a canvas ball as I had seen many kids play with them. Every day, I waited for my father to return in the evening, and he would come empty-handed. The ball was too expensive for him to buy. And look at you now.'

'I would give tuition to students in MSc when I was doing my BSc. That's how I paid my way through. Look at you. Money is not a problem for you. You can do whatever you want, but you hardly study.'

'At least study enough so you can do the maths when you have to run a grocery shop.'

'I cleared the IIT exam, but my father couldn't afford the fees.'

'Always be grateful for what you have instead of always wanting more.'

## THE WORLD RECORD

In class eleven and twelve, we have a subject called Socially Useful Productive Work—SUPW. You are supposed to do something useful and then write it up in a project report.

Everybody is doing something. Going to a slum. Conducting a blood donation drive. I just don't know what to do. Two days before the deadline for submitting the project, I get hold of an old issue of the *Illustrated Weekly of India*. It is a special on the changing face of Indian advertising over several decades.

I cut it up with scissors and gave it the semblance of a project report. It looks good, but I can't find the faintest justification for why the project is socially useful.

The day comes when our class-teacher, N.L. Singh, settles down to examine our projects. He starts making all kinds of faces while reading mine. It is as I had feared. The thing is a no-go.

He looks at me disapprovingly, and I have a brain-fade moment before I let loose one of my tall ones.

'I am planning to break a world record, sir, and the proceeds will go to charity,' I tell him with a poker face.

'What, what?' he asks.

Nobody has let loose such high-voltage gas at him before. But I am a serious bugger with a serious mien.

'Skipping, sir. I want to break the world record in skipping,' I say in hushed tones, so that Shivendra Bahadur doesn't catch what I am whispering in the teacher's ears. I don't want him sniggering and guffawing. The *Bahalwa lambi goli dee* kinds.

N.L. Singh looks at me with awe. Then he announces to the class that I will address them on a world record I aim to break. I did not see this coming. I look at my teacher hesitantly. He insists. I get up.

'I am planning to break the world skipping record. At the moment it's around thirty-three thousand continuous skips, according to the Guinness Book of World Records. I can do ten thousand continuous. I am practising more,' I say.

There's a hushed silence. Nobody is sniggering. They are taking me seriously. Oh my god.

'But I need help in terms of off days and leniency in attendance so that I can practise harder,' I continue.

I am actually a rope skipper. I skip daily. But the maximum I have done at one stretch is three thousand skips.

Word travels far and wide in all sections after my speech.

Even guys from the science section come up to me and wish me all the best. My teacher takes me to the principal, Father Thomas. I regurgitate my nonsense. Father Thomas nods his head sagely. 'Tell us what help you need,' he says.

'Just some help with attendance, Father. I will be practising a lot,' I say.

'Okay, tell us what you need in writing,' says Father and dismisses me.

I never give anything in writing. N.L. Singh passes me in SUPW on the strength of my skipping endeavour.

## SANGAM, 1984

My friend Devesh Sahay has got a present from his uncle in Italy. It's a rubber dinghy with paddles, to be used in a swimming pool. It comes with a foot-pump to inflate it, and you spend hours pushing the damn thing with your foot.

We have the bright idea of rowing it all the way to the Sangam, the confluence of the rivers Ganga, Yamuna and the mythical Saraswati. It is one of the holiest pilgrimage spots for Hindus, and every twelve years it hosts the Kumbh Mela, where millions of Hindus congregate from all over India and abroad.

We take the dinghy to the fort on the Yamuna and pump it up. Devesh, Neeraj Roy and I work it by turns.

Finally, we hop into it with our paddles and row all the way to the Sangam. Going is easy as we follow the current. We jump out and bathe at the holy spot. The water is not too deep. While returning, the dinghy gets a puncture, and air escapes it in one furious burst. We paddle hard to reach the shore. It's just about two hundred metres upstream, but the going is tough. A boatman jumps into the water and comes swimming over to us. He pushes us upstream as we continue sitting in our dinghy.

We are all grateful. It is quite an effort. He doesn't even take any money from us.

## THE BLESSINGS OF SWAMI VIVEKANANDA

My extended family on my mother's side has been associated with the Ramakrishna Mission for several decades. By this I mean they have been influenced by the writings of Sri Ramakrishna and Swami Vivekananda and other monks, and have even interacted with some of them.

My uncle Girish was a friend of Swami Ranganathananda for several decades. In his last years, I presented Swami Ranganathananda with my uncle's biography on Boshi and Gertrude Sen, *Nearer Heaven Than Earth*, and he spoke to me for several minutes about his friendship with Girish uncle.

My mother's IAS-officer uncle, S.S.L. Kakkar, knew Swami Ranganathananda in the 1950s and wrote about him in his memoirs.

I took to Vivekananada on my own. By the age of eighteen, I had devoured all the literature available at the Ramakrishna Mission. I was a volunteer at their ashram in Allahabad and spent several weeks working as a handy boy there.

My guru, the late Swami Prabuddhabanda from Moradabad, had himself joined the mission as a brahmachari in the 1950s. He later left the mission and started his own ashram in Moradabad. One day, out of the blue, he asked me whether my family had any association with Swami Vivekananda.

I went and asked my grandmother. The year was 1984. She said that as a ten-year-old in Meerut, her father had delivered milk to Swamiji for several days. This may have been after Swamiji became famous as Vivekananda, or earlier, when he was a mendicant roaming the country. Both seemed equally likely.

My grandmother's younger brother, however, had no memory of this. He said he did not remember his father telling him any such story. But my uncle Girish remembered his grandfather telling him that he had heard Swamiji speak either at Meerut or Agra, as a kid.

Girish mama's long association with Boshi-da is another link to Swamiji. Boshi-da was a disciple of Swami Sadananda, the first disciple of Swami Vivekananada. Sadananda was the stationmaster at Hapur railway station when he met Vivekananda—before he became the Vivekananda that we know. There was such a glow on his face that Sadananda was entranced and renounced his worldly life that same day to become his disciple. Later, as Sadananda, he would say that he only followed a 'devilish pair of eyes.'

When Sadananda was sick in the 1920s, Boshi-da and four others used to look after him. They were called Sadananda's 'kukurs' (or dogs) as their lives were devoted to him. It was Sadananda who told Boshi-da that the life of a monk was not for him and that he would have another calling. Boshi-da ended up founding the Research Institute at Almora, where he met my uncle—the district magistrate—in the 1960s.

## DRILLS FOR INDIRA GANDHI

Four classes have been choreographing special drills for over a month. Classes nine, ten, eleven and twelve. Our school's hundredth anniversary falls in October 1984. Prime Minister Indira Gandhi has been invited to be the chief guest.

We are doing a special kung fu drill, and a fourth-dan black belt master has been taking us through some katas. But he never once does them himself. One day, after a particularly strenuous session, we urge him to show us some deadly black belt moves. It gets to a point where the chorus of voices suggests that if he doesn't oblige, we will likely brand him a fake. So, with great reluctance, he decides to show us how a back somersault is done. After some preparation, he does one and lands flat on his back. It's quite a heavy fall, and he lies there for a few minutes while we struggle not to snigger and laugh. He doesn't turn up for the next few days, and when he does return, he is very sheepish.

Meanwhile, our subject teachers have been told to become drill instructors for three hours every day. Mrs Amrita and Mrs Gandhi, our English teachers, are out in the field, in the sun, watching us go through our paces. The prime minister is due at our school on 4 November. We have a dress rehearsal on 29 October.

Indira Gandhi is assassinated on 30 October.

## YOGA CAMP, 1984

I am at a yoga camp in Pithoragarh with Swami Bimalananda. I have got to know him through former deputy inspector general Manas Mukherjee.

I spend fourteen days in Pithoragarh learning yoga. Our hotel is at the top of a hill, within walking distance of the temple of Ulka Devi. I go there every day and sometimes sit for hours. Some days, tears well up in my eyes as I sit quietly on the steps, listening as a certain lady sings a devotional song.

Bimalananda-ji has been observing me. He asks me why I cry. I say I don't know. He says it's good that I cry.

Nobody knows Bimalananda-ji's age. Estimates vary from seventy-five to ninety, but he doesn't look a day over sixty. The tales he has to tell, of pilgrimages to Kailash Mansarovar in Tibet in the pre-Independence days, are simply riveting.

It is while I am at the yoga camp that Operation Blue Star takes place, and Bhindranwale is killed by the Indian Army. Bimalanand-ji says that he fears for Indira Gandhi now. He says that the prime minister has to be careful for the rest of the year. I don't know if his knowledge of yoga has anything to do with his gloomy forecast, or if it's just plain foreboding.

Certain Indian Army units revolt as a consequence of Blue Star, and the Sikhs in all other army units come under observation. As I travel back to the plains by bus from Pithoragarh, four Sikh soldiers in uniform are seated at the back of the bus. They are going home on leave. I recognise one of them as my NCC instructor in school, who was transferred out a few months earlier.

There are police checkpoints on the way from Pithoragarh to Lohaghat and after that, on the route to Haldwani. At every checkpoint, the soldiers are told to alight and are patted down and inspected by the state police.

I start feeling embarrassed for them. Whenever they are called down, I go with them, and shoot the breeze to try and take some of the tension out of the air.

At Haldwani, when we part, my NCC instructor says, '*Main samajh gaya tu kya kar raya si. Acha munda haiga tu.*' I know what you were doing there. You are a good kid.

## THE MONK OF BENARES

I meet him in Benares in 1985. Swami Brahmheshananda is a monk with the Ramakrishna Seva Ashram in the city. He is also a doctor, and has been treating patients for more than four decades. I often land up at the mission in Luxa in Benares. I enjoy chatting with the monks, and they invariably invite me to have lunch with them.

Once, the conversation with Swami Brahmheshananda turns to Volume I of *The Complete Works of Swami Vivekananda*. It is one of my all-time favourite books, an ocean of spiritual ideas and insights.

Swami Bramheshananda tells me he was standing on a railway platform one day, when a man threw a copy of the book down from a train. 'It landed at my feet. The man said to me with disgust in his voice, "Reading this, my son wants to become a monk." The train pulled away. Nobody picked up the book. So, I picked it up and took it away. And after I finished reading it, I became a monk.'

He tells me the story without any flourishes. Like it is an ordinary happening, without much to be read into it.

When I read the book, I too nearly become a monk.

## A GOAT, A BULL, A BUFFALO, A MONKEY, A DOG, A CAT AND A COW

I am sitting at Dashashwamedh Ghat in 1985—a year in which I make several trips to Benares because of the ill-health and subsequent demise of one of my father's aunts.

I have befriended a travel agent from France. We sit together, watching the Ganga flow by as we discuss life at Dashashwamedh Ghat. He has brought tourist groups to Benares more than a dozen times, and the little free time he gets, he comes and sits on the steps of the ghats.

At some point, I ask him why he loves Benares so much. He says, 'This is the only place in the world where I can share space with a bull, a buffalo, a cow, a monkey, a dog, a goat and a cat as if it were the most natural thing in the world.'

He points to each one of the animals around us.

The observation stays with me for a long time afterwards.

## NILADRI MAHARAJ

### MONK, FRIEND, COUNSELLOR

'What are you doing here sitting on these steps?' asks Niladri Maharaj. 'I have seen you many times. You come in school uniform during school hours and just sit here?' I have been coming to the Ramakrishna Mission's mandir in Mutthiganj, Allahabad, for several weeks now, and sitting on the steps leading up to it after a period of meditation.

Niladri Maharaj is a monk at the mission.

'I don't know,' I say. The truth is that I find great peace here.

This simple interaction starts a deep friendship.

From 1983, until I graduate from Allahabad University in 1988, I remain a frequent visitor to the mission. Sometimes I even bunk school to go there. I form lasting friendships with many monks in the order, some of whom I am still in touch with. One of my classmates even joins the order shortly after graduation.

I volunteer sometimes at the bookshop and relish my interactions with the monks. When Niladri Maharaj comes to stay in an ashram on the banks of the Ganga for lengthy sessions of meditation, I visit him frequently on my scooter.

Once, when I take it into my head to have a career as a deep-sea diver (I am known to have these strange impulses), it is Niladri Maharaj who comes home and counsels me. Later, he is transferred to Calcutta and serves at Seva Pratisthan. At some point, he leaves the order and becomes untraceable. Some say he has become a Buddhist monk and lives in the Himalayas. I don't know.

## MY FIRST JOB

In 1988, my father gets posted to Calcutta as the director of the National Airports Authority. All the airports in the eastern part of the country fall under the ambit of his office. I have just graduated from Allahabad University in English, history and philosophy and want to prepare for the civil services examination.

Actually, the 'preparation' for the civil services never happens. I use it more as a ploy to shut people up when they ask, 'What are you doing?' People always have to know what you are up to! I even enrol for a master's in philosophy at Jadavpur University. I buy all the books, attend classes for a few months, hit on many of my classmates, and then drop out altogether.

Unlike Allahabad University, Jadavpur has so many cliques within a section that it is a virtual landmine to negotiate. Each new student is looked upon as meat to be poached by the different groups. After a while, I get sick of reading philosophy and travelling the two hours from Dum Dum to Jadavpur by bus.

One day, I notice an advertisement by a company looking for salesmen. It is a walk-in interview. The company, Ranutrol, sells electronic typewriters, and another of its divisions, Ranutrol Hansa, sells bathroom fixtures. The office is the same, so one room has plumbers in it, and the other has graduates selling typewriters.

The senior manager interviewing me asks why I want to join sales and not study further. For want of a better answer, I say that I would rather get some experience in the field for the next few years, and then perhaps reach a marketing position, with the bonus of earning all through this time.

I don't know why they give me the job. The manager is too poker-faced for me to tell whether he finds my answer impressive. I think he just wants someone who can speak a little bit of English.

I remember a few things vividly about the two months or so that I worked there. I sell an electronic typewriter within the first week of joining. It isn't really a cold call. I sell it to the son-in-law of one of my father's colleagues. He runs a firm trading in rubber products, near Howrah Bridge. The whole of Calcutta is divided by the company into two zones—south and north. Though I am in the southern team, I sell this typewriter in the cusp of the northern area and they claim it. A big showdown happens between the heads of the two zones as to which team can claim the sale. Competition is tough, and my boss berates me for calling in the sale without informing him. He says, 'We could have shown a South Calcutta address and claimed the sales for our team.'

One of the northern team members has a murder rap going against him and sometimes has court appearances to make in between sales calls. But he still chalks the maximum number of orders week after week. Some call it luck. The truth is, he does more sales calls than three salesmen combined. His daily call report lists a minimum of ten calls per day. He is simply superhuman.

Our office is on the fifth floor of the Stephen Court building on Park Street. The entrance is from the back. If I feel hungry, I can always go to Flurys and have a pastry or a sandwich. Which is seldom, as my salary is a paltry Rs 1,500.

One day, an irate customer walks into our office. His machine is causing problems. It wasn't serviced in time, and the daisy wheel is jamming. He is in such a rage that he keeps shouting at the salesperson who has sold him the machine. My colleague Shantanu doesn't quite know how to handle the situation. When the customer has briefly exhausted his spittle, I butt in. 'That's a nice pair of shoes you are wearing, sir. Can you tell me where you bought them? I want to buy them too,' I say.

This totally defuses the guy's anger. He starts chatting with me about how the Chinese handcrafted shoes from a particular shop in Tangra are the very best in Calcutta. Shantanu thanks me profusely afterwards.

The third incident I recall from my time there is being out on a sales call with a senior salesperson. They would often team us with a senior so we could learn a few tricks of the trade. We land up at a public sector undertaking (PSU), where I happen to know a senior management person. I spill this fact to my senior, and his eyes light up. After having scored an order so soon after joining, everybody looks at me like I am the guy with the Midas touch.

But I am embarrassed about being a salesperson. And hesitant to introduce my colleague to the PSU manager. 'What will he think, that I'm just a salesman,' I comment to my colleague. I go in to meet my acquaintance alone.

We exchange pleasantries. I nearly don't bring up my real purpose. 'Oh, I was here and noticed your nameplate! What a coincidence, uncle!' I begin. No leads are generated, of course.

When I emerge from the office, my colleague sits me down on a bench nearby and gives me a few life lessons. I don't remember much of what he said except the general drift of it. 'Listen, Aniruddha, no work in life is below one's dignity. You think selling is low. But everything is sold. There's no difference between selling a 747 jumbo and a typewriter. You just have to know your product and the customer's needs.'

## MY FIRST NOVEL

All of 1990, I slog on my first novel, *A Crack in the Mirror*. I write it in long hand, taking photocopies every ten pages. I am worried it will get lost. My parents think I have gone mad. Instead of preparing for the civil services, I have given up my sales job and started writing a novel.

It takes me a whole year to finish it. And an additional month of typing in WordPerfect to get it on a floppy disk—those big floppies before the advent of the three-inch ones. I send the manuscript to several publishers and get rejection letters from twenty publishers or so in the UK. I even give the manuscript to my uncle Jagdish, who is visiting Calcutta, but he can't make head or tale of it. It is a simple love story set in a university campus.

I talk to the publisher David Davidar about *A Crack in the Mirror* some years later, and he remembers having read it. He comments, 'But nothing happens in it.' So that was the end of it as far as Penguin India was concerned.

Another publisher, Rupa, shows interest, and so does Writers Workshop in Calcutta. Ultimately, Rupa publishes it in 1991. I remember the first few copies coming in by post and my mother opening them. She is very pleased. I don't think she ever reads the book, though.

# ARE YOU FROM ALLAHABAD?

Allahabad never abandons those who have lived there. In the 1970s and 1980s, while I was growing up in the city, it was a lazy town. It still is. However, in a story that it shares with all Indian cities, the big bungalows are now disappearing, and builder flats are replacing them. The old gentry has dispersed around the world, and the easiest way to take care of ancestral houses is perhaps to sell them. Most of these houses are on long lease, and converting them to freeholds costs a bomb.

When I visit the city now, there are areas that are unrecognisable, but some have managed to remain the same. The old city is by and large the same as it was. Chowk, Johnstonganj, Mutthiganj, Loknath ki Gali and many other areas are in a time bubble. Allahabad is a town of lawyers and doctors and retired people. There is still no industry, and you have to get out if you want a career of any sort. Still, the city has a charm that can only be understood by those who have lived there.

Allahabad has a tendency to leap at you in unexpected places. I was once travelling to Tokyo, and I thought the person sitting next to me seemed familiar. I peeked at his passport, which he was fiddling with, and saw the surname Dwivedi. That was when the penny dropped. He was the brother of a classmate of mine from class nine! We had a nostalgia-fuelled flight.

Another time, when I was having breakfast in Oslo in 2002, I looked at a lady sipping coffee at the adjoining table and decided she must be a Pakistani. I had met many Pakistanis there over the past few days and assumed erroneously that she was from our neighbouring country. Then, voila! She got a call on her mobile phone, and I heard her speak in Hindi. If there's one thing I can recognise across rooms and banquet halls, it is people talking in the Allahabadi accent.

'Excuse me,' I said to her, 'are you from Allahabad?'

She was stunned! She turned out to be Menaka Das, an actress living in London at the time, who had grown up in Allahabad. Her elder sister had taught in my school. We spent a most memorable afternoon walking around in Oslo and talking about our memories of Allahabad and common friends.

The city has also taken me out of jams. The Indian bureaucracy, at one time, was heavily populated by Allahabadis. The university there catered to students from all over UP and Bihar, and if you came from a small town, you would later appropriate the identity of the city as it perhaps made you 'cooler'. When I got into legal trouble during the Atal Behari regime, I was often helped in unexpected ways by people from Allahabad.

## VISA BLUES

It is 1997. This is the first time I am going to the UK, and I apply for a visa. I collect it from the British embassy at Chanakyapuri, but I don't check it for details. I just assume that the embassy has given me a multiple-entry visa, like I have asked for.

I am chasing a few stories in London. I travel to Paris over a weekend. When I come back by the tunnel, the immigration officer has his moment with me.

'Where's your visa?'

I stare at him blankly. *You duffer, you can't recognise the British visa*, I think.

I open the page for him. 'Here it is.'

He looks at the visa. He looks at me. 'Where is the visa?'

Is he playing with me? What's the problem with him? I am showing him the visa, but he won't budge from his point. 'Where is the visa?'

Then I look at it closely and see that it's a single-entry visa.

Fucking shit.

By some stroke of luck, I manage to talk my way out of the situation. It's not as though it's a parking ticket, mind. But you can still speak to immigration officers and explain your problem to them.

Being a journalist helps. A press ID helps too. As does a letter from the British Tourist Authority addressed to me. I explain, patiently, that if he sends me back to Paris, I will have a problem on my hands as my luggage is lying in a London hotel. The officer calls his superior. I explain the whole thing again. They let me into the UK with a warning stamp on my passport.

I would never have got through in a post-9/11 world.

## ESHA ON THE WAY

I am in London in mid-1997. There are no cell phones. To call home, I use one particular booth outside the Tottenham Court Road tube station.

On one such call to Noida, I sense Reema is reluctant to tell me something.

'*Kya baat hai?*' I persist. What's the matter?

'Nothing,' she says.

'No, it's something,' I say.

'I am pregnant again,' she says.

There's a moment of silence.

'That's such good news,' I say.

'You are okay with it?' she asks gingerly.

'Why would I not be okay?' I ask.

'Can we afford another kid so soon? I heard Maa-ji saying that we should have planned better,' says Reema. Our first-born, Rhea, had arrived in December 1996. The next one, if all goes well, is due in February 1998.

'You don't plan these things. They happen. I am happy,' I say.

'So, you are okay?' she asks again.

'Of course I am!' I say.

And that's how I hear about Esha.

I wanted to call her Tara, but the proposal was shot down by my mother. She wanted the child to be named after Goddess Parvati.

On subsequent trips to London, whenever I crossed Tottenham, I would look at that phone booth and feel a tug of emotion each time. Sometime in the last decade, however, the phone booths were rearranged because of the expansion of the tube station underneath. I miss that booth.

## WHERE IS RHEA?

It is 1998, I think, and my elder daughter, Rhea, is about two. Home is an apartment in a high-rise in Sector 21, Noida, on the seventh floor. One Sunday evening, Rhea is nowhere to be found. My mother and I look all over the house, but she just isn't there. We are scared that she may have walked out while the door was open. A five-year-old girl next door is her favourite didi. But Rhea is not with her. We always keep the doors to our balcony locked. Did we forget to lock the door? I step onto the balcony at least ten times to check. But Rhea is not to be seen anywhere.

The buildings in the complex are interconnected on all floors. We knock on the doors of all our neighbours, as well as those living in the adjoining towers, but there is no sign of her. By then, we are in such a state of panic that all our neighbours have started looking for her too. Where can a two-year-old have disappeared?

After a long and fruitless search, we come back home. And that's when my mother finds her. She has wriggled her way inside our hollow divan and is sitting there, grinning, with a bottle of Johnson's baby oil in her hand. She had been rubbing oil all over herself and her clothes.

While we were shouting her name out loud, she had kept as quiet as she could. She knew she was doing something naughty and didn't want to be caught out. She is the same even now!

## THE VIDEO CAMERA

While my daughters were growing up—I mean the early years, sometime in the late 1990s and about two years into the millennium—there were no cameras on cell phones and video cameras were costly. I would often borrow a video camera from my colleague and friend Neerja Jaitely at *Outlook* magazine to shoot videos of my daughters, as I was concerned that I would never have moving images of them. I must have shot for a few hours over several weeks in 1998.

I then forgot all about it, and the cassettes languished in a box when we moved house. Sometime in 2011, I discovered them, and it became a task to transfer the footage from the tapes. It proved difficult because of the size, but I finally managed and put all of it on a pen drive. Over dinner that day, I asked my daughters and wife whether they wanted to watch a movie I had made. I wouldn't tell them what it was. I said, however, that they would have to pay two hundred rupees each. My daughters used to earn pocket money by giving head massages to their grandparents and to me.

But they all balked. I played so many pranks on them that they thought this was another one of my tall ones. No matter how much I said they'd enjoy it, they wouldn't budge. And I was adamant that without the price of the ticket, no movie would be screened.

Finally, Reema cracked because it was becoming boring sitting around in the sitting room, and the kids agreed to pay a discounted sum. I then played the footage for them. They were absolutely riveted. There was a sequence of me trying to scare baby Esha by growling at her. But she wouldn't flinch at all. No matter how many angry noises and sentences I threw at her, she ended up grinning at the camera!

I was trying to locate the footage the other day, but it's disappeared again.

# PART II

'*Tehelka* is a giant anti-corruption machine.'

—Anonymous

# STARTING AT *INDIA TODAY*

It is 1991. I have come to New Delhi on a sales trip. I am partnering with my uncle, who has a handicrafts unit in Moradabad. I help him get bulk orders for gifts. I also have a job interview with Dabur India. I don't get the job, but that evening, walking around Connaught Place, I see the big *India Today* hoarding in F Block.

I have an impulse to just saunter in and ask for a job. So I walk in. By this time, Rupa has come out with my novel. My plan is to send a copy of the book to the copy editor and then maybe chat with him. The receptionist at *India Today* is a woman called Zola. She is of a helpful disposition. She summons a girl from the desk. Devika comes out to meet me. I explain my purpose.

'Could you please pass on this novel of mine to the copy editor? Could I meet him?' I ask.

Devika goes back in. After about half an hour, Tarun Tejpal comes out.

'Yes,' he says. He has a poker face. I am at a loss for words. He has already seen a copy of my novel—the publisher sent it to him for review. I don't know whether to push him for a review in *India Today* or for a job. I explain to him that I am looking for a job on the copy desk.

'Come tomorrow for a copy test,' he says.

I return the next day for the test. It's on IBM's Atex system. I finish the test in one hour and leave. I come back the next day and sit in the reception. Devika comes out and says that I will be informed of the result in some days. But I insist on meeting Tarun.

'He hasn't come in yet,' she says.

'I'll wait for him,' I say. Devika shrugs and goes back in. The editorial department is on the second floor, and nobody can enter the office without having to go through the reception. Tarun walks in. I smile. A phone rings on Zola's desk. Zola tells me that Tarun is busy today. I go away, disappointed.

The next day, I am in the reception once again. Unsolicited visit.

The routine is repeated. Devika comes out. She says Tarun is not in. I keep waiting. Tarun comes in finally. He is always late for the edit meeting. He sees me, but doesn't say a word.

One day, after the edit meeting, he calls me in. He tells me to join in a few days. My starting salary will be Rs 2,500.

That's how I start my career in journalism at the desk in *India Today*. Tarun tells me many years later that he hired me so that he could walk through the reception without having to see me!

## MY FIRST BYLINE

I have filed a story idea for a photo feature on the National Security Guards (NSG) with the *India Today* news coordinator. I have some contacts within the NSG, and they will allow me to do a story and photo shoot with them. Another senior journalist, who is acquainted with the director general of the NSG, B.J.S. Sial, also gets permission, and we do the story together.

Pramod Pushkarna is the photographer assigned to us by the magazine, and we shoot some training sessions embedded with the commandos. One of them says, and I think quite correctly, 'We are like nukes. The ultimate back-up.' Eventually, this would become my first story with a byline.

It doesn't happen in the usual way, though.

I write up the story and send it to the desk without adding my byline, assuming that they will put my name alongside the other reporter's. When I find out that they have removed my byline and left in just the senior reporter's name, I am very upset. I go to my copy editor and explain the situation, and he probably goes to Dilip Bobb, the deputy editor. Dilip ultimately lets my byline stand alone. It's not a feeling I'll forget in a hurry—the excitement of seeing my name appear in newsprint for the first time.

## TOXIC WASTE IN DELHI

In 1994, I join the team at *Down to Earth* magazine after being interviewed for the job by Anil Agarwal and Sunita Narain. The office is in East of Kailash, in south Delhi. Later, it will move to Tuglaqabad, near Batra Hospital.

Uday Shankar, who will go on to become the president of the Walt Disney Company, is my boss at the science and environment monthly. He heads the team that brings out the State of India's Environment report, and sends people all over the country to chase stories. Max Martin and I do a story on toxic-waste disposal in Gujarat and Maharashtra, which has me travelling for weeks together through industrial estates. That's where I get my first taste of investigative journalism.

My nosiness leads me to a story about a PSU in Delhi that is disposing of untreated gypsum in a landfill in west Delhi.

The chemicals leach through the landfill and contaminate the groundwater, affecting the communities around the area. I chase a dumper truck all the way to the landfill and watch it dump the gypsum. I go ahead and collect about two kilograms of the material, wrap it in many layers of newspaper and store it in my brother's Contessa car.

I then get it into my head to confront the director of the PSU. He has the guards chase me out of the factory premises. Fortunately, my car is parked only a kilometre away, and I scramble to it like a bat out of hell.

I dump the gypsum under my desk in the office, and everybody comes around to have a look. I want it chemically analysed, but no laboratory will do it at a reasonable cost, so that's the end of that.

One day, a Norwegian donor drops in to the *Down to Earth* offices, and Sunita Narain brings him around to our floor. Very sweetly, she asks whether I can show him some of the chemical stuff I have been fooling around with. In my eagerness to impress, I scoop up a bit on my plastic pen and hold it straight up to the guy's face so he can take a good look at it.

He arches back. His face reddens, and he beats a hasty retreat.

## NIGHT-TIME READING

In 1994, in between quitting *Down to Earth* and joining the *Financial Express*, I have a month off. I speed read about seventy books in that month. I have always felt that if you cannot read at least one book a day, you are doing things wrong. The only time I consciously stay away from reading is when I am working on a novel. I find it interferes with my writing.

Then again, between 2001 and 2014, I don't read much. Where earlier my night-time reading used to be novels and non-fiction, for these thirteen years, it becomes affidavits and writs and replies to applications and other legal stuff, as I am involved in several court proceedings. There is the Justice Venkataswami Commission of Inquiry, the army court martial proceedings, the metropolitan courts and, of course, the high courts and the Supreme Court.

On an average, I am physically present in one court or the other once a week. If I tabulate the days, it adds up to 676 days, or nearly two whole years of my life. I am discounting here the many days I spend preparing for the court proceedings, giving statements to police officers and spending time at the offices of my lawyers.

My lawyers soon begin to call me half a lawyer. I gain valuable insights into how the system works—the sheer obtuseness of it still surprises me. My memories of musty court rooms, the idiosyncrasies of various judges, the victories (many) and the defeats (none so far) are still sharp. I will never be free of them.

I spend more than a month on the witness stands of the Justice Venkataswami Commission of Inquiry, a period when the law officers of former prime minister Atal Behari Vajpayee come after us with a vengeance, and fantastic tales are spun. All these tales wind up as my night-time reading!

## WHEN IN KOREA...

I am in Seoul in 1994 doing a business supplement for the *Financial Express*. I am travelling with a business executive, let's call him PV. We are at the global headquarters of Lucky Goldstar. One thing

I've learnt about Korean corporate executives: they always carry diaries and notepads, and they wear ties.

They can be a little intimidating. You can even time their rituals. When their notebooks will appear in their hands. What kind of questions they will ask. What they will serve. They are most curious to know about the different states of India and invariably know more than you about certain state policies.

At this particular meeting, PV and I start bantering in Hindi. We play a game of predicting when what will happen. In how much time the senior VP will come in. What they will serve us, and so on. We don't hold back on the use of our extensive vocabulary. We even add a few choice abuses. Every time we do that, I notice that two of the managers at the meeting perk up and smile.

After the meeting is done, these two managers escort us downstairs, and we engage in a last few polite exchanges.

'You should come to India soon,' I say politely.

'Oh, we study there. We are just visiting Seoul ourselves,' says one of them. The other nods.

'Oh, studying what? Where?' I ask, surprised.

'We are about to finish our course in Hindi from JNU,' says he. The other nods.

They look at us with mischievous smiles.

I don't know where to look.

## THE GHOST WHO WALKS

Being a part of the inaugural team of *Outlook* in 1995 is enervating. Vinod Mehta starts the publication with Deepak Shourie. He had founded *The Pioneer* in the early 1990s, and reporters who joined him early on had built their reputations because of Mehta's habit of giving credit where it was due. He was never constipated about giving bylines for work done.

*Outlook*, under him, becomes a reporter-driven organisation. Reporters' ideas get primacy. Mehta is also very fair. He may call you to his room or talk to you ten times a day, but that is by no means an indication of proximity. Journalists realise this after the first few meetings.

Part of Mehta's daily routine is to walk around on the second floor, where the desk, the reporters and the photo section are located. He slouches and roams noiselessly, rarely talking. If you're engrossed in typing something on your desktop, it may be a while before you notice him peering at your screen from over your shoulders.

Sometimes he makes a comment, and more often than not, he walks away before you have time to react. A lot of reporters are under pressure to be doing something when he is on the floor. Like pretending to be researching something or making calls or reading some stupid report.

Some of the women reporters who have joined recently are caught unawares and literally jump out of their seats when they become aware of his looming presence. Some develop excellent peripheral vision, minimising their internet browsing windows as the ghost walks the floor.

## FARE MOST FOWL

In the first year of *Outlook* magazine, I do a story that brings me a lot of silent backlash. We test cooked chicken samples from a KFC outlet in Delhi, La Brasserie in the Le Meridien hotel, the coffee shop at Ashoka Hotel, and Nirula's. The analysis is done by the Food Research and Analysis Centre (FRAC) at the Federation of Indian Chambers of Commerce (FICCI) in New Delhi. The tests detect MSG (monosodium glutamate) levels as high as 1.37 per cent in the food from KFC. The Prevention of Food Adulteration Act, 1954 (Part X111-64B) clearly specifies that the total glutamate content of ready-to-serve food should not exceed 1 per cent. The then KFC managing director has been claiming that the MSG content in KFC's chicken is between 0.1 and 0.2 per cent.

Chicken from the two other eateries shows significantly less MSG levels and in the case of Nirula's, a total absence. While the chicken from Le Meridien (La Brasserie) has an MSG level of 0.67 per cent, Ashoka Hotel's count is as low as 0.136 per cent.

In my copy, I quote Professor T.D. Dogra of the forensic department in the All India Institute of Medical Sciences (AIIMS): 'Though MSG has a toxic rating of one, medical journals often describe a link between MSG and a distress syndrome after consuming Chinese food.' Quoting from *Clinical Toxicology of Chemical Products*, a publication by Williams and Wilkins, London, Dogra defines the syndrome as similar to that which occurs when subjects are treated with monoamin oxidase inhibitors when challenged by foods rich in tyramine: burning sensations, facial pressure and chest pain. These same symptoms are known to have been provoked in human subjects by large oral doses of MSG. In fact, 50 per cent of the subjects responded to doses of 4 g or less. A kilogram of KFC chicken, on the other hand, on the basis of the FRAC's analysis, would have 13.7 g of MSG.

Soon after the story is published, the Bangalore Municipal Corporation issues notices of closure to KFC on the basis of excess MSG in their food.

The *Outlook–FRAC* analysis also shows the presence of aluminium in KFC's chicken sample. I quote Dr S.K. Saxena, the director of FRAC, and others, in my piece: 'While the KFC sample showed aluminium traces, the other three samples tested negative.' The main medical point of contention here is the acceptable limit of aluminium ion absorption by the human body, because of the metal's implication in certain neurotoxic disorders. According to A.P. Hirano of WHO's environmental health hazard division, 'individuals with chronic renal diseases are highly susceptible to aluminium ion absorption.'

KFC, however, contests the story. They are critical of the methods that we have adopted for collecting the samples and even question FRAC's competence. They also claim that samples from any Chinese restaurant would show a higher level of MSG.

KFC has Perfect Relations as their public relations firm, and as soon as KFC receives a questionnaire from us, Perfect Relations starts calling Vinod Mehta frantically to get the story dropped. But Sandipan Deb, the business editor, and Mehta remain firm. What works in our favour is that we got the analysis done at FICCI's own laboratory. KFC can hardly raise questions about an industry body.

It is a story I look back at with a deep sense of satisfaction.

## A NEW CONNECTION

It is 1996, and I am settled in my job at *Outlook*. My parents live in Lucknow, and my mother's primary occupation is hunting for a suitable girl for me to marry.

My parents advertise in the classified matrimony section of the *Times of India*, and arrange meetings for me in Delhi, where I meet girls chaperoned by their families. Nothing fruitful has transpired in any of those meetings. Families often cite their misgivings about the earning potential of journalists.

One such meeting looms again. The girl is coming with her father. It is a lunch meeting in Connaught Place. We are supposed to meet in front of Wimpy, a fast-food restaurant in the outer circle opposite Palika Bazar, and get a meal somewhere.

I see them walking towards me. A father and his daughter. When we meet in the walkway, the sunlight falls on her face. She is radiant. I know instantly that I want to marry this woman. Her name is Reema. She says yes after our second meeting.

## NIGHT OUT

Sometime in early 1996, a documentary production team from Swiss TV lands up in India to make a documentary about the emerging nation. They are referred to me by a Swiss journalist friend, Suren Erkman, who did a stint at *Down to Earth* while I was working there in 1994.

I fix interviews for Eric Burnand and Chantal, his new wife, and make friends for life. They give me some money for helping them out, and I am finally able to afford a desktop computer. I immediately start writing a novel that has been whirring around in my head for some time. It's the story of what happens during the course of a single evening, and is set in New Delhi in the mid-1990s. I call my novel *Night Out* and send it to Gillon Aitken, the celebrated London agent of Salman Rushdie and Sir V.S. Naipaul, among others.

Gillon writes back saying that he is not impressed, but if I write something else, I am welcome to send him the manuscript.

I undertake a journey to Vaishno Devi in Katra, hoping the Mother will do something to help my efforts along. She is still ignoring me.

## TSANGBOSCHE

T. Narayan and I are covering the tragedy on Mt Everest in 1996. Sixteen people have died on its slopes. We have flown to Tsangboche to await the return of the climbers, particularly those who are part of David Breashears's expedition: Ed Viesturs, Araceli Segarra (the first Spanish woman to climb Everest) and Jamling Tenzing, son of Tenzing Norgay, the first person to ever climb Everest along with Edmund Hillary.

The Breashears team has been shooting on the slopes of Everest with an IMAX camera. Their film will release in theatres worldwide and do great business.

I troop several kilometres up and down, meeting sherpas who have climbed Everest more than half-a-dozen times each. They lead simple, frugal lives in their villages and go up the mountain to provide for their families. I meet Ang Rita, who at this point has already gone up the mountain eight times. Also Apa Sherpa, who will go on to break all records on the mountain.

The weather turns bad at Tsangbosche, and Narayan and I get stuck in an inn with Breashears and his team. I end up spending a lot of time with Breashears, Viesturs and Tenzing. The inn is a ramshackle construction. You have to shit into a hole in the ledge and watch your shit drop down the mountain slope. In the dark, you can't even do that.

I cosy up to Breashears because he has booked a helicopter back from Tsangbosche to Kathmandu and has promised to give us any spare seats available.

Finally, the weather clears and the helicopter manages to land. It is one of those lumbering Russian choppers with space for about twenty people. As I sit by the window, I see some kids come up to the fuel tank and turn on the nozzle for the aviation turbine fuel. They take off with a few buckets, possibly to use for cooking or heating purposes. Then the chopper takes off, and I am afraid the whole flight long that the kids haven't turned off the nozzle of the tank, that we are leaking fuel as we weave through the valleys. But we reach Kathmandu safely!

## THE HOUND OF THE BASKERVILLES

There is one crazy story that Prashant Panjiar and I do after roaming around in the interiors of Uttar Pradesh, where, for the previous few months, some animals have been picking up and making off with kids. This reaches fearful dimensions when, from three districts of UP—Pratapgarh, Sultanpur and Jaunpur—thirty-two children below the age of ten are reported missing and eaten by animals. Rumours start swirling about giant, vicious wolves or greyhounds or jackals that are doing the rounds of the villages and picking up easy prey.

On the one hand, it's tragic, since so many babies have been snatched from their mother's arms. On the other hand, the stories themselves are beginning to seem like they are fit for the pages of science fiction.

The UP government commissions a group of hunters from Madhya Pradesh. They come with some old muskets and sit in machaans. Then comes the news that kids have been snatched from some nearby villages, and we land up there immediately. Once the villagers learn that we are reporting on it, they start telling us bizarre stories of how a monstrous kind of a man is behind all of this.

'He has red lights stuck on his face,' one says.

'His leg have springs attached to them,' goes another.

Septuagenarian Surya Kant Mishra barges into our hotel room and insists, 'Huzoor, it's about ten feet tall and can jump sixty feet. It has got four light bulbs on its head and one each on its feet. The lights come on once it jumps, and they are so bright that if you look into them, you are blinded for two days.'

Panjiar and I look at each other incredulously.

On top of the tragedy of half-devoured human bodies, there's a grim, dark humour at play here. Even in the face of such tragedy, it is hard for us to keep straight faces. This definitely counts as one of the most bizarre stories I have ever done.

In the end, 2500 wolves are decimated in an attempt to control the deaths.

## AN ALTERNATIVE

It is the year 1997 and the first World Polypathy Congress is being organised in Delhi by Professor P.R. Trivedi, chairman of the Indian Institute of Ecology and Environment. Alternative healers and practitioners from all over the world are gathering in the Indian capital for the congress. I am there to cover the events and people—from the most mundane to the zaniest. I meet healers from all over who were once in other professions but somehow got drawn into the field.

It's all quite surreal and extremely interesting.

After I file my story, I receive over thirty letters from readers asking for contact details of the healers I mentioned in it. Apart from letters, there are dozens of phone calls to the magazine's landline, from people wanting to talk to me. But the bulk of interaction with readers is through the post.

This is way before the Indian government takes to endorsing alternate modes of healing. I realise there are so many people out there who are suffering from various diseases and really want to know about these cures, having lost much of their faith in allopathy. The story gives me a new perspective on human suffering and on the power of words to move people, when used in the right way.

If I have to pick one of my stories for the kind of special attention it got in the pre-social media days, it would be this one.

## MURDER MOST FOUL

A sudden and dramatic crime story draws us to Lucknow and to our editor Vinod Mehta's alma mater, La Martiniere, a 152-year-old institution with an impeccable reputation. The assistant warden and physical-training instructor, Frederick Gomes, has been ruthlessly murdered.

About a month earlier, an air pistol converted to a .22 had been discovered with one of the student boarders at the school. The weapon had circulated among the students, the asking rate for purchase being a measly Rs 500. Students in class ten and eleven were handling the weapon out of curiosity, and when it was finally discovered and confiscated from a student by Gomes, he beat him black and blue before taking him to the principal, Elton D'Souza. The principal then expelled five students and deposited the weapon with the district magistrate. The matter was considered to have been effectively hushed up and settled and out of the public eye. But on Shivratri in 1997, Gomes was fired at eighteen times in his home. He took four bullets in the chest, one in the leg, two in the back, and the fatal one in the temple, from a .763 Mauser and a .38 pistol.

Doing this sort of an investigative story for the first time is a challenge. It is especially complicated because I have to interview kids, most of whom are, of course, shitting their pants. Some I interview with the consent of their parents, and others are only too eager to talk to me.

I stumble through this new territory, ruffling a lot of feathers. The principal is infuriated with me as I end up talking to some kids about what exactly happened. It opens up a Pandora's box that nobody can close afterwards.

## MEETING OMAR

There is one interview I remember quite fondly.

It is my first trip to Kashmir as a journalist, in 1998. The winter games are on. There is a skiing trail from Gulmarg, and they get a lot of journalists to promote the ski run.

Omar Abdullah is just about launching his political career. This is his first major interview to a media house. He tells me about his school and college days. He is from Lawrence School, Sanawar, an elite school near Shimla. He went to the UK after finishing his

BCom at Sydenham, Bombay. He tried securing a job there for eighteen months, to no avail. He returned to India, worked at the Oberoi Hotel, met and married a Hindu girl, Payal Singh.

Is he worried about the conspicuousness of a Hindu wife in polarised Kashmir?

He ponders for a bit before saying, 'I don't know whether it will impact me politically, but if somebody brings it up, they should be exposed for what they are.' I am impressed with his candour.

He himself had a baptism by fire. Two years earlier, at a civic reception in Jammu, the organisers had suddenly announced Omar as a speaker. Recollecting the occasion, he says: 'Both my father's and my wife's heads went down. They thought, "God, he is either going to stammer or speak in English!" But I spoke for three minutes in Urdu, and I guess that's when I felt I might be a natural. That it was in my blood.'

## BRIAN LARA'S DIATRIBE

I start my career in sports reporting in 1996, during the cricket World Cup that Sri Lanka ultimately wins.

It is my first time covering any sport at all, and it's purely by chance—one of our sports reporters has just resigned from *Outlook*, creating a sudden vacuum, and Tarun Tejpal assigns me to replace him. I am a reluctant participant, though I soon take to my job. But it begins badly.

When I land up to cover my first cricket match in Gwalior (India vs West Indies), I don't even know that reporters are assigned a separate press box. I find myself in a different tier, sans company. It's only when I find out that they are passing around special lunch boxes at the end of the match that I finally discover that the reporters have a dedicated press box of their own, and that I am going to enjoy some privileges out there!

An interesting thing happens in the second match I cover, in Pune. I am, at this time, also pursuing a feature on how the Indian diaspora is represented in international teams—for example, the West Indies has Shivnarain Chanderpaul, and Kenya has a whole gamut of Indian origin players.

In Pune, the Kenyans upset the West Indians in a crazy match. Batting first, they are dismissed for 166 runs in about 35 overs. Everyone is expecting the mighty West Indies to knock off the runs needed in about 25 overs, but the Kenyans end up bowling them out for 93 runs! Chanderpaul is the top scorer with a paltry 19 runs, and Brian Lara falls for just 8 runs.

All part-time players, the Kenyans are ecstatic at their victory. Having seen a lot of me during the tournament because of the feature I am working on, they invite me to their dressing room to celebrate. While we're there, Brian Lara walks in, congratulates them, and launches into an unguarded diatribe against his team and his management. I am just standing there—a fly on the wall.

Amidst quick batting tips to the players, Lara confesses that losing to a Black team like Kenya is hardly as bad as losing to the 'White' South African team. The Kenyans sense a mood and want Lara to keep talking. He seems piqued and is forthcoming with some interesting confessions. He rues the fact that the West Indies team isn't at its best: there are problems in the team, and they have a bad management, he says. Some of the players do not even talk to each other. They just stick to their own hotel rooms, with minimal socialisation. In fact—he comes out with it rather brazenly—Carl Hooper missed the series not because he has malaria, as people have been led to believe, but because he is fed up with the team's situation.

Lara also confides that there is an inherent management bias against players from Trinidad and Tobago, the home of Gus Logie and Larry Gomes. He says the management doesn't like it when players from there make it big. He is an eyesore for them, he says, and he feels a distinct lack of encouragement and appreciation, even at public events like press conferences. He says that messages are sent from the green room to stall his swashbuckling approach, and it sometimes ruins his game.

He is quite vehement in his outpourings—'You know, if you have a good team and a bad management, you can maybe get along. But if you have a bad team and a bad management, you really get fucked. After this defeat, I think they'll be forced to sort out some of this shit.'

I quickly file a story about his comments, and it spreads like wildfire. International wires pick it up. My story is essentially about Lara's comments on the problems of West Indian cricket, but the international media pick up on his comments on the South African cricket team, which are racist in nature.

Subsequently, the West Indies team manager Clive Lloyd calls a press conference in Pakistan. Brian Lara sits alongside him and apologises for his comments. Vinod Mehta is terribly excited about the traction this story receives. On the other hand, I begin to understand the nature of media, and how one story has the ability to morph into an entirely different one.

## KEEPING WICKETS

During the Indian cricket team's 1997 tour to South Africa, a match is organised between the Indian and the South African media. It takes place at Centurion Park on 8 February, a day after Zimbabwe's historic win over India in the rain-affected Centurion match.

I keep wickets. Right next to me, at first slip, stands the legendary Sunil Gavaskar. There are also big shots like Mohinder Amarnath, Yashpal Sharma and Maninder Singh playing for our side. It's the first time I have come into direct contact with these cricketers, whom I adulated growing up.

I tell Yashpal Sharma that I have kept wickets before, but that is, of course, a complete lie. I goof up majorly at the stumps and get shouted at by Maninder. '*Aai Aniruddha, ki karreyasi? Naak katwaiga.*' What the hell are you doing? You'll make us lose face!

Sunny looks at me and says reassuringly, 'That's the typical Punjabi way of playing cricket. Instead of making you comfortable, they have flustered you now. That's how the Pakistanis play cricket. They are at each other's throats all the time.'

'What about sledging the batsman?' I ask.

'Only Sarfaraz used to do that. The others would just talk amongst themselves,' he replies.

I suddenly have the golden opportunity to solve an eleven-year-old riddle.

'What did David Boon say to you as you walked past him when you got out at 90 in the tied test match in Madras in 1986?' I ask, rather apprehensively. Aussie aggressiveness was at its peak, and it must have been something really bad, I have always imagined.

'I think he said "well played",' recalls Sunny.

The great are respected everywhere. And by everyone, even competitors, I think, though it's an anticlimax.

I then share my little secret with him. 'This is the first time I've kept wickets in my entire life. Actually, I did it just to be able to stand next to you,' I say.

Sunny just smiles and winks at me.

## COOKING WITH JIMMY

During the same tour, I discover that 'Jimmy' Mohinder Amarnath has a hidden talent: his culinary skills are beyond reproach.

Before the final at Durban, he puts his skills to good use at a dinner hosted by South African journalist Katherine Kane. Among the guests are quite a few vegetarians.

Jimmy enters the kitchen with great gusto, declaring, '*Humare vegetarian bhai bandhuon ke liye kuchh banana padega.*' Gotta make some arrangements for our vegetarian friends here.

He then proceeds to rustle up aloo gobi, aloo fry, steamed rice and dal.

A Bangladeshi doctor settled in Durban says it's the best aloo he has had in his entire life.

## MAMU'S IDLIS

Wherever you go, you find some little-known traditions that have been practised for ages. The Indian cricket team, for instance, has the following peculiarity: they always have on hand some local who can cook or get authentic Indian food for them. They always keep this hanger-on around them. Sometimes these are good characters, and sometimes unsavoury ones.

They call these men 'mamus', and go to their homes to eat. Every tour has a different mamu, as does every country. The mamu cooks the food and brings it to the team. On occasion, the culinary offerings are elaborate, catering to the whims and fancies of players from different parts of the country. Some are vegetarian and some non-vegetarian, and the mamu has something for everyone.

In general, the team is always on the lookout for vegetarian and home-cooked food. Some of them are a bit stingy and don't want to spend money on eating out. But mostly, I think, the mamu tradition has to do with the fact that during long tours, like in Australia and New Zealand, the players are away from home for long periods of time and are genuinely homesick.

I remember one particular mamu, a good guy. Nayan Acharya had come to New Zealand as a twelve-year-old and worked his way up to becoming the owner of a chain of restaurants called Mr India. He used to turn up at the nets in shorts and run after stray balls. I especially remember the idlis he organised during a dinner break in Taupo. And Sachin and Sunny Gavaskar swore by his chicken jalfrezi.

I find the way the Indian team treats their mamus extremely amusing. The mamus, in turn, want attention in terms of autographs and photos, and they bring their own guests and let them take photographs with the poster boys of Indian cricket. At least till 2003, there was a whole mamu culture that went with the Indian cricket team. Whether it persists now to the same extent, I don't know.

## CATCHING THE BIG FISH

The behaviour of certain journalists in the press box during the India–South Africa one-day series in South Africa in 1997 sets me off on a scent that results in reverberations far greater than I can imagine.

I see a few journalists betting on the matches, but that's not very surprising. What really gets me is that they are doing it from the press box, even while the match is on. There are dedicated landlines that you can have assigned to yourself for a certain fee, and one of the reporters from a major Indian daily is yakking away on the phone to bookies pretty much the whole time. My ears perk up, because it's not only odd but also pretty much one of the most unethical things you can do as a journo. I know they are in the box by day and are chummy with the players in the evening, hanging around in the dressing room and listening in on team conversations.

I begin to wonder if anything stops them from passing on inside info on the team and individual players to the bookies—who is playing at what place in the order, who is injured, and stuff like that. The whole thing seems fishy.

I sniff around a fair bit and speak to ex-players, commentators and others, who start revealing things off the record.

As I keep digging, I smell a big story.

What holds the investigation in place is that I am working at a magazine, not a newspaper. I don't have the pressure of daily deadlines. And I have two luxuries on my side—I have time to go after what I want and I don't have to be pally with the cricketers like the newspaper reporters feel pressured to be. This is what enables me to pursue my special stories.

I don't even know that I am suddenly donning the role of an 'investigative' journalist. The term is bandied about a bit too much these days. I still feel that any story you spend time on, and research, can become an investigative story, even if it's structured as a profile or a feature.

All I know is that I have to get to the innards of this story. I have to absorb the matter and look at it from all possible angles. There are your own discoveries. And there are people telling you things. And your story stands propped on the edge of all these.

In the case of this particular story, the penny drops. I have an instinct. I follow it. And I find that there are many more things to find. It starts up the great game.

## THE GREAT GAME

Manoj Prabhakar's interview to us in 1997 splits the cricket world wide open.

This is the time when *Outlook*'s main rival *India Today*, a fortnightly, is making the shift to becoming a weekly. The story needs meticulous planning, and Krishna Prasad and I have been working on it since February. We are trying to come up with the best possible opener for it. Finally, the chance comes, and we break the cricket match-fixing story in June 1997. We time the story so that it coincides with *India Today*'s first weekly edition. That, really, is Vinod's call.

In my interview with him, Manoj Prabhakar talks about how, from the time he joined the Indian cricket team, he was sucked into groupism because of the confusion over whether he belonged to the north group or the west. He talks about money changing hands and decisions being taken solely on the basis of betting. Once, in 1991, he recalls, he and Sanjay Manjrekar were walking off the ground in Sharjah because of poor light, when they got a signal from the team management to play on.

Manoj's interview opens a can of worms.

He says he was offered up to Rs 25 lakh by a teammate to play below par against Pakistan in the 1994 Singer Cup in Sri Lanka. He says he refused vehemently, but the offers kept coming. He speaks of Mongia passing him instructions to go slow.

It is an exciting time for me. This is the first time any media house anywhere in the world has claimed that match-fixing and betting exist in cricket. It is the start of the whole cricket match-fixing saga.

Everybody thinks we are running after a mouse, that we are playing to the gallery. Nobody has a clue how deep the rabbit hole runs. And when it comes out, it almost looks like we are in the wrong, and the story is not correct. The Board of Cricket Control in India (BCCI) sues us for a sum of Rs 5 crore. Many years later, they will withdraw the suit, as subsequent events and investigations reveal that we spoke the truth. This is my first proper legal case. At that time, I have no idea there will be so much more!

The story has tremendous impact. The Pakistan Cricket Board holds an inquiry and finds certain players guilty. The Indian board investigates and bans some players. The Central Board of Inquiry (CBI) starts an inquiry as well. When the match-fixing stories around Shane Warne and the Waugh brothers become public, the loose ends begin to be tied up.

By the time the year is up, everyone has an idea of how widespread match-fixing in cricket really is, and we feel vindicated.

## INDO-PAK BHAI-BHAI

The follow-up to the match-fixing story proves intense. Someone reaches out to me. It seems a twenty-six- or twenty-seven-year-old Pakistani cricketer has a huge dossier on match-fixing that he has compiled on his own because he is being victimised by his country's cricket board. Because of certain names that he has taken internally, the board has gone against him, as have a few senior players.

I am supposed to contact a Pakistani-origin British citizen in London, who runs a talent representation agency that works with a lot of Pakistani players. From Delhi, I establish contact with the man. Syed, as he is called, meets me in London. He eventually reveals that the cricketer in question is Rashid Latif, the wicketkeeper and captain of the Pakistan team. I remember he was vice captain in the tournament for the Mandela trophy in 1995 in South Africa.

I meet Latif, and he makes a series of revelations which create a big stink in India. He openly names Azharuddin and Jadeja, and says Kapil Dev is 'the biggest gambler of all'. I prod a bit further.

'I know a lot of things. I have the minutes of the Pakistan Cricket Board meeting that mentions the bookies involved in the whole thing—Dawood Ibrahim, Mukesh, Rahul bhai.'

More shit comes out.

'There is an Indian television commentator who is a big bookie. In the last World Cup, he was commentating at a match involving India. But outside the studio, he was more concerned about the outcome of the Pakistan match. An Indian player told me this.'

The Latif interview takes forward Prabhakar's original story, and leads to the reopening of cases against some Indian players.

An Indian cricketer named in the story subsequently gets a fax from Latif that he thinks absolves him. A few months later, under the pressure of a lawsuit by the BCCI, Vinod Mehta gets panicky for a while, and wants me to get Latif to give one more interview clarifying certain issues. So I arrange to meet Latif in the UK, where he is playing for a minor club. He has been provided a house and a car by the club, and he insists that I stay in his house. Even though the story had caused him a lot of embarrassment, he doesn't try to avoid or distance himself from me. He never gives me the clarification Mehta desires, but subsequent events make it unnecessary. This encounter begins a long friendship between us, and during the ICC mini-World Cup in Dhaka, Latif presents me with his playing bat, which Mehta promptly pinches and displays on his editor's desk for many years.

## CHAI WITH JUSTICE CHANDRACHUD

After suing us for Rs 5 crore, it suddenly dawns upon the BCCI to initiate a formal inquiry in the wake of the story we have broken. Headed by former chief justice of India Y.V. Chandrachud, the investigation's modus operandi is to call a lot of ex-cricketers, commentators, players, journalists and board officials for a session over tea, and some general chitchat.

On 17 October 1997, I am part of a meeting at the official inquiry into the Indian betting controversy, in a first-floor room of the Cricket Club of India (CCI). The executive secretary of the board, Sharad Diwadkar, asks me whether I have brought along Rashid Latif's tapes.

Yes, I have. Why wouldn't I, I wonder.

'If the justice desires to listen to the tapes, he may do so,' I say.

But Chandrachud appears least interested in the tapes. He offers me tea instead. The conversation meanders aimlessly for twenty minutes. Towards the end, I remind him of the tapes. He seems uninterested.

'One can ascribe all sorts of motives to Latif for making those statements,' he says.

He shouts at the board official who has set up the audio system so that he can listen to Latif's tape. 'Why do I have to care about what some Pakistani has to say about Indian cricket?'

To another journalist who asks the same question, he responds, 'Who knows whether it's Latif's voice or somebody else's?'

There is no grilling on the veracity of the story, no questioning regarding my sources or any queries about my methods. I am crestfallen at his nonchalance. I try to prolong the conversation by regaling him with one fact after another. It is to no avail. The guy's not interested in anything I have to say. If my stories weren't entertaining, the meeting would have been over in less than ten minutes.

This obviously isn't the way I expect an inquiry of such magnitude to unfold. The betting scandal is massive; I expect a serious inquiry, at the very least. But this is a wishy-washy thing. I give up expectations of any meaningful outcome from the process.

Chandrachud doesn't fail my expectations: he exonerates everyone at the end of the farce.

## MARK IS THE MAN

In the world of cricket, I am as curious about the men behind the scenes, who play outside the field.

That is how my interest in Mark Mascarenhas grows. Boss of WorldTel and the commercial custodian of Sachin Tendulkar, Mark is the first guy to realise the importance of TV rights in the era before Lalit Modi. He is a financial genius. And I follow his movements in the shadow of the law with some interest.

We start off on the wrong foot, as it so often happens. I am working on a profile of Mark, and as part of my research, make a few calls to his associates. News of these calls carries to Mark. And he is none too pleased.

One day, I get a call on the *Outlook* landline. It's Mark, and he threatens me left, right and centre. 'Just see what I do to you,' he shouts. It's an infuriating conversation. I go and tell Vinod about this encounter.

'Those who bark never bite,' says Vinod. 'Just forget about it.' And as it happens, I do.

I eventually do a profile of Mark Mascarenhas, and he likes it despite there being certain unflattering things in it. He speaks to me again, despite remembering having shouted at me. I appreciate the guy. He has it in him to be nice and get past the unpleasantness between us, I think. He makes time and speaks to me at length. He doesn't take the criticism to heart that much, and we end up having a most convivial conversation.

We will go on to become great friends.

When I leave *Outlook*, I become a member of the founding team that is to bring out *Cricket Talk*, a magazine owned by Mark. I stay for only a few months and quit, much to his chagrin, before the magazine launches.

## SACHIN AT TWENTY-FIVE

A few months after Mark's profile is published in *Outlook*, I find out that Tendulkar is holidaying at Mark's house in Connecticut. I ask Mark whether a photographer and I can fly to the USA to do an extended interview there. He agrees immediately, promising he will get Sachin to say yes. So Prashant Panjiar, who is the photo editor, and I fly to the US, and I get to do a long interview with Sachin.

It is obviously a bit of an intrusion. He is there to relax, play pool, ride the yachts, shop, spend time with his daughter, enjoy quality seafood and sleep a lot—all the things he doesn't get to do often. This is right after his explosive innings in Sharjah, where Steve Waugh predicted that by the time he was finished, Tendulkar would be second only to Bradman. I remember Mascarenhas telling me that Sachin always delivers if you set up a stage and expect him to perform, whether in cricket or at pool at three o'clock in the night (as he is doing while on vacation).

A documentary on Tendulkar has just been released, and the great Don Bradman himself has been recorded saying that he considers his style 'much the same as I used to play ... I can't explain it in detail, but it's just his compactness, and his stroke production and his technique ...'

Sachin is bashful when I mention this. 'It is the greatest compliment I ever got. I called my parents, my brother, to say this is what Bradman said about me. It thrilled me.'

Sachin has a different image from most other sportsmen. He has maintained his dignity for the most part, refusing to be baited by tobacco and liquor companies for endorsements, instead conforming to the high-adrenaline image of an athlete. He speaks to me about his coach, Ramakant Achrekar, to whom he gives a lot of credit. He tells me that he would get four or five sessions in the nets everyday, with Achrekar standing behind him. 'I would be tired. He would place a one-rupee coin on top of the stumps. Whoever got me out would get that. If no one got me out, I got to keep the coin. I would be totally focussed on not getting out.'

He gradually opens up enough to speak about his debut innings against Pakistan in 1989. 'I was tense. Whatever I had expected to happen didn't happen. I felt after that that I wouldn't be able to handle international cricket at all. But I was hoping for another opportunity. I made up my mind not to lose my wicket. I got 59. When I got back, I remember saying I don't know any reason why I can't do it again.' In the series, he never took a backward step, not even to short pitched balls, as Richie Benaud has since observed.

It still rankles Sachin that his stint as captain wasn't garlanded with his own match-winning performances. He reflects that captaincy is an aggregate of the team's performance and that his low phase made him mentally tougher. He wasn't as disappointed to lose the captaincy as was made out—'I didn't go into depression or anything. For me, playing and winning for India is the ultimate.' He says he thrives on the respect of his peers and strives to maintain long-term performance rather than short-term goals.

It is refreshing to catch him in a relaxed mood after the intensity of Sharjah, and have him share his feelings and memories of younger days. At fourteen, he recounts, Dilip Vengsarkar had presented him with a Gun and Moore bat. He also tells me that Anjali, his wife, is much more involved in watching the game now than she ever used to be.

Panjiar obviously gets lots of pictures of Anjali, but Sachin makes me promise to not use any of them. I agree in good faith. Back in Delhi, Panjiar informs me in a hushed tone: 'Vinod has seen all the pictures. He wants to run the picture of Anjali.'

I panic. The printing form of the magazine is a day away. Vinod is not ready to relent. 'It's our scoop. Nobody has seen his wife's pictures. Why should I spoil some good visuals?' he insists.

'This wasn't what I agreed with him,' I say, trying to fight back. Panjiar doesn't push back—he has submitted the pictures and says it's the editor's call. Even Tarun Tejpal, then the managing editor, can't convince Vinod to drop Anjali's pictures.

I still regret not having had the courage to inform Sachin in advance that *Outlook* was going full monty. He might have had a chance to convince Vinod by calling him directly.

Expectedly, when the pictures come out, Sachin is mad at me. He calls me in the office, and we have a one-hour telephone conversation, interrupted only by his lunch. He derides me about going back on my word, and I apologise about a million times, pleading that I'm just a minion and Vinod is the boss. I propose putting him on the line to Vinod and letting the two of them have it out, but neither Vinod nor Tendulkar agree.

'I have nothing to do with Vinod,' Sachin tells me.

For a long time after that, Sachin doesn't speak to *Outlook*.

The story also creates a lot of heartburn among Mascarenhas's rivals. They send insinuating letters to the magazine about how I enjoyed Marc's hospitality at his Connecticut home. But Prashant and I did our interview and vamoosed. We didn't even drink tea at Mark's place.

## HIDE AND SEEK IN DHAKA

After Krishna Prasad and I break the match-fixing story in 1997, we are treated as pariahs by the cricketing establishment. For a while it becomes difficult to get media accreditation from the BCCI to cover matches. They put up hurdles each time. As a result, I don't get accreditation for covering the ICC mini-World Cup in Dhaka in 1998. Instead, colleagues from other publications smuggle me into the stands using their identity cards.

The grounds are always a coveted place to be in because one can not only chat with other broadcasters and senior journalists but also with the cricketers on the field, as well as, of course, the physios of the different teams, who have all the gossip.

But the ICC has different plans for me. Tipped off to my presence in the grounds, they send two officials to look for me. The idea is to humiliate me by expelling me from the stands. For the duration of the match, I am helped by local journalists and others to evade the ICC hunters. My friends keep shifting me from one stand to another. I leave the grounds with about an hour remaining of the match. I don't want anything to happen that might embarrass *Outlook*.

In the years immediately after our exposé, the BCCI remains vicious. Jagmohan Dalmiya rules the roost, and he can be vindictive. It is the first time I realise the price to be paid by reporters if they do stories against the establishment. The cricket boards are like ostriches, their heads stuck below the ground. Many senior sports journalists, including the likes of Dicky Rutnagar, chastise me in private for exposing journalists who were consorting with bookies from the press box. A small minority stands beside me in this time: Sabysachi Sarkar from the Anand Bazar Patrika (ABP) group in West Bengal, Pradeep Magazine at the *Pioneer* and Ashish Shukla, who used to write for the PTI and, earlier, for the *Times of India*. In fact, Sarkar nearly loses his job with the ABP group for supporting me with quotes about the involvement of certain journalists.

## MIANDAD AND THE PAKISTANI DRESSING ROOM

In 1998, during the ICC mini-World Cup in Dhaka, I become friends with former Pakistan team captain and then coach Javed Miandad. I enjoy every moment spent with him. At some point, he writes columns for us in *Outlook*. We pay him Rs 10,000 for them. Of course, he can't write to save his life, but he shares his thoughts with me over the phone in Urdu, which I then translate into English. The *Outlook* accounts department hands over to me the receipts Miandad has to sign each time, and it is a constant battle for me to get him to do so.

This familiarity with him gives me easy access to the Pakistani cricketers and allows me to hang out with them informally. Sometimes, when I happen to find myself on the same flight as them, I get to play card games with Miandad, Salim Malik and Ejaz Ahmad at airport lounges. One such game is at the Calcutta airport, where a delayed flight has us playing rummy in the lounge for an hour while listening to Ejaz Ahmad's raunchy Punjabi jokes.

Later that year, the Indo-Pakistan Test Series takes place in India. At the Chennai test, which Pakistan wins in spite of a gut-wrenching-second inning score of 136 from Tendulkar, Miandad calls me into the Pakistani dressing room to dictate his thoughts about the match. While we are talking, Wasim Akram gets out, and when he returns to the dressing room, he sees me sitting with Miandad. He isn't at all pleased.

After the game, I walk up to the prize-ceremony area and get talking to the Pakistani players. I still remember Salim Malik taking me aside purposefully and saying that Tendulkar should have seen India through, especially after taking them so close, back pain or no back pain.

## BIGGER THAN BODYLINE

The match-fixing scandal breaks the hearts of millions of cricket fans. As we become the outcasts of the Indian press, we are constantly on the lookout for a chance to prove ourselves right. That chance comes unexpectedly.

I am in Dhaka when Sakyasen Mitra, a Bengali journo working for the Hyderabad-based *Eenadu*, hints that he can help corroborate Manoj Prabhakar's story that he had been offered money to perform badly in the Indo–Pak match.

I am very interested.

Mitra claims he overhead most of the conversation with Prabhakar from the next room. He was working for the Calcutta-based newspaper *Aajkal* back then, and had access to the room adjacent to Prabhakar's at the Lanka Oberoi, where Prashant Vaidya and Nayan Mongia were staying. Vaidya was an old friend; Mitra's father had coached him while he was part of the Bengal team. 'I don't remember the exact room numbers. They were these L-shaped rooms with a connecting door,' Mitra tells me.

'That day, I was sitting with Vaidya and a few others, including a journalist from *Ganashakti*. Usually when I walked into Vaidya's room, I would peep through the adjoining door to see if Sherry (Siddhu) was there, because I was a little friendly with him. But he wasn't. Manoj was alone in the room, reading a magazine.' The incident in question happened a few minutes later, when Mitra was back in Vaidya's room.

'I heard him shout,' says Mitra. 'He shouted, "What do you think you are doing? Can you buy me out in an India–Pakistan match? No amount of lakhs can buy me out. How can a person in your position do this?"'

I am elated. Our story has meat, and our source stands vindicated. I still have to speak to Vaidya. Yes, he says, when I call him, Mitra is a friend and used to visit him regularly. Yes, the rooms were next to each other, and yes, the adjoining door was open all the time. It was very possible to hear whole conversations through it.

I decide to speak to Prabhakar, who corroborates the sequence of events. 'I am glad that there is some corroboration for my story. At least the people who said I was talking in the air should be silenced.' He sounds relieved.

Mitra evidently hadn't realised the implications of what he had heard until much later. 'The Chandrachud inquiry was so fraudulent. How many journalists who went on the '94 tour were invited to depose?' he asks. Mitra also says that his father, who was the curator of the Eden pitch, had repeatedly advised Indian captain Azharuddin not to bat second on that pitch during the semi-final match of the 1996 cricket World Cup, as it almost guaranteed a loss. Azharuddin went ahead and chose to bat second anyway.

I ask Mitra why he kept silent for almost two years. He tells me that he was taking a sabbatical and hoped to return to cricket reporting. He was afraid that 'the cricketers won't talk to me if I spoke the truth. Also, the issue became so big that I was a little scared. But now, with the new developments, it's become a very vital issue. The truth has to come out.'

It has indeed become vital. Subsequent stories on the scandal have carried David Hookes's confirmation that Mark Waugh and Shane Warne accepted money from a Madras-based bookie. The time is right for more revelations.

I immediately decide to run the story, and the BCCI is forced to institute an inquiry into the matter. The cat is now officially out of the bag.

## FRANCE, 1998

In 1998, I land up to cover the football World Cup without any FIFA accreditation. Priyaranjan Das Munshi is the president of the All India Football Federation (AIFF). I try to get a last-minute accreditation through him, but he isn't helpful, though he did get it done for a few journalists from Calcutta. The AIFF secretary,

Kedar Nath Mour, who Munshi does not get along with, turns out to be helpful, and hands me a bunch of tickets for different matches. He even gives me six tickets for the inauguration ceremony. I refuse them, saying I'm alone, but he insists, saying he doesn't know what to do with them. A bunch of his friends haven't landed up, and the tickets are useless to him. I take them without realising their value at the time.

I give two of those tickets to some friends of friends. It's a windfall for them. But I'm still left with three. The next day, I read in the papers that tickets have been stolen, and the agency handling the ticketing system for FIFA is paying $250 for a single ticket for the inaugural event, as they're running short themselves.

Of course I'm tempted. I have three tickets and am on a starvation allowance from *Outlook*. So I land up at the agency, promptly hand over my three tickets and walk off with $750. I shift to a better hotel than the B&B I have been in, where the basin is next to the bed.

However, there's a sting in this tale. When I reach the stadium, there are hordes of fans lined up along the route, willing to pay $2,000 per ticket! I kicked myself—if I had waited, I could have made a cool $6,000, but it was not to be.

I consider selling my own ticket and watching the match on TV, but eventually decide against it. Brazil is playing the opening match, and I want to see Ronaldo on the pitch at least once!

## THE ENGLISH PACK

While covering the football World Cup in France in 1998, I make a stop in Marseilles, where English football hooligans have rioted and are holding pitched battles against the police. There, I get to see first-hand the dynamics of the British tabloid press.

I am friends with several British reporters, and travelling with my friend and brother-in-arms Shekhar Bhatia of the *Evening Standard* gives me a ringside view. I find that if you move with the pack, you share everything with the pack. For instance, when the Marseilles police arrests several British fans and they are produced before the local courts, very few of the British hacks can understand the proceedings in French. But those that do painstakingly translate for everybody else. A few who arrive late are given the full lowdown.

There are solo operators as well. The pack won't share a single piece of information with them. And yet, as an outsider, I am allowed to pick from their quotes and other material without restraint. I am friends with someone in the pack, and nothing else matters.

One thing that unites all these tabloid journalists is the swiping of expense vouchers. It is standard practice. The pack, or parts of the pack, will land up at a restaurant for dinner. They have a boisterous meal, and when the bill arrives, everybody chips in to pay. Then they get into an argument with the waiter and the manager, and while some of them go back and forth over some flimsy point on the bill, a few others go to the counter in the back and whack the bill book of the restaurant. After leaving, they tear off the empty invoices and distribute them among themselves. All to file rigged expenses!

## MEETING VIV RICHARDS

At *Outlook*, our covers on Tendulkar pile up—they will run into double digits eventually, I'm sure. Once, we have an entire issue dedicated to him, edited by Krishna Prasad. I end up doing an interview with Viv Richards for it.

I spend a marvellous evening with Viv in Bombay, at Neena Gupta's house. Their daughter, Masaba, is a child.

I ask Viv about his first meeting with an allegedly nervous Sachin, in Australia, where Sanjay Manjrekar is believed to have introduced them. Viv says he sympathises with Sachin's lack of form after he became captain. He is quite candid about the fact that his own batting suffered tremendously when he was made captain of his team. 'A captain had to be manager, father, everything.'

Viv says Sachin has now shifted into a different mode, learning to become more consistent than Brian Lara, his sole rival for the title of the world's greatest batsman. Viv's all-time favourite player, however, is Sunny Gavaskar, though he does say in the same breath that Sachin is 99.5 per cent perfect, and he would pay to see him play. He tells me a story about being on the same flight as Sachin, who was on his way to a charity match in London. Viv assumed he would disappear into the first-class cabin. But he came and sat with Viv and chatted with him the entire trip. 'What's amazing about that kid—I call him that because he is so tiny—is that he is always willing to learn,' says Vivian, laughing.

I really enjoy talking to Viv. He tells me about playing without a helmet, recounts the time fast bowler Greg Thomas got under his skin, making him hit 140—he speaks freely and lucidly, witty and convivial at the same time. He confides that he used to have a long mirror back home and practised shots in front of it, sometimes all night, imagining bowlers running up to him and bowling. He tells me that if he were ever to be sledged as a player, it would only motivate him to concentrate harder on giving it back through his game.

It is one of my most treasured interviews. I can remember, with complete clarity, talking to him as he sat there in his shorts. For those of us who grew up watching Viv, there can never be another like him. One can only imagine the havoc he would have caused in the Twenty20 format!

## TRAVELS WITH IMRAN KHAN

In 1999, during the cricket World Cup in England, I spend two full days with former Pakistan cricket captain Imran Khan. I travel in the back seat of his car, discussing politics and cricket with him. He takes me to two of his party's fundraising events, and I hear him speak about his vision of a corruption-free Pakistan. He is honest, sincere and driven. When my *Outlook* colleague, photographer T. Narayan, and I land up at his then father-in-law Sir Jamie Goldsmith's house to photograph Imran, he comes out with his son Sulaiman and poses for us.

Three moments stand out for me in my interaction with him. On one occasion, he has just come out after a round of commentary on an ongoing match, when former England cricketer Ian Botham walks by. They exchange a glance and a greeting. There is much history in that moment. In 1996, Khan won a libel case instituted against him by Botham and Allan Lamb for calling them 'uneducated racists'. Botham's suit further took offence at Khan accusing him of 'ball tampering'. The court ended up ordering the two to pay legal costs of £500,000. I ask Imran how he feels about Botham now. He replies: 'I never had anything against him. In fact, I sent him several messages to drop the whole thing, but they unnecessarily dragged it on and then they were ordered to pay the court fees as well. To be frank, I felt sorry for both of them.'

In 1992, when Pakistan won the cricket World Cup in Australia under Imran's captaincy, he did not once thank his team in his victory speech. As a cricket fan, it remained a mystery in my head, and I am not going to let the opportunity pass. I ask him about the incident, and he says, 'It was an oversight. I wasn't expecting to speak. Also, I never was much of a speaker. The hospital thing was also swirling in my mind. It was not arrogance.'

The third moment that stands out is when, sitting in the back seat of his car, I ask him whether he sees South Asia ever becoming a union like the European Union. Actually, whether he would like to see it happen. He categorically brushes aside the idea. 'There is no need for it,' he says.

## AN EMBARRASSING MOMENT

In September 1999, I accompany the India A cricket team to Los Angeles for a series of games they are playing against the Australia A team. The matches have been organised by the US Cricket Association.

The Indian team is led by V.V.S. Laxman and includes Virender Sehwag, Ashish Nehra and Mohammed Kaif. Sehwag is yet to make his reputation as India's main demolition man. The Indian coach is former Indian player K. Srikkanth. I spend hours on the flight with Sehwag, trying to understand him. Sometime later, I listen to Ian Chappell going gaga about Kaif's straight bat. I tell him then that the unsung star here is Sehwag—I have never seen anybody hit a cricket ball harder than him.

Sehwag goes on to play a few cameos in Los Angeles in a rain-interrupted match. He thrashes the Australian bowlers all over the park. One of the balls crashes into the bicycle of a Los Angeles city cop on patrol duty, and he walks into the stands to have a look at the player who is causing such havoc!

But it isn't the cricket that I remember so well from the trip. It is the embarrassment I subjected myself to. I still go red in the face when I remember the episode. We travelled to Los Angeles via Bangkok. There is a long stopover there, and I go shopping with former India team players Maninder Singh and Yashpal Sharma, who are acting as umpires for the series. There are others with us, but at some point, they all go back to the hotel to be well in time to make the coach to the airport.

I hang out a little longer, trying on trousers. Then, on the way back to the hotel, I get stuck in one of those notorious Bangkok jams. As a result, by the time I reach the lobby of the hotel, nearly all the players are already in the bus, and a few stragglers are clearing their bills at the counter. I have to scurry up to my room, pack with superlative speed, come down and clear my bill, even as the coach is kept waiting just for me.

I have never again had to move in such a hurry, I am sure, as I did then. I must have taken all of ten minutes before finally walking towards the bus, but I can feel all the players glaring at me. Srikkanth smiles at me and says, 'Ah, the media is late as usual.' Laxman is also sitting in the first row. He doesn't say anything. He doesn't glare or smirk. I apologise to the first-row occupants and rush to the back to hide myself!

For a while after this, whenever I bump into Srikkanth, he ribs me about my sense of time. His own son is named Anirudh and so he has a soft corner for me, I presume.

# BETS, LIES AND DECEIT

The match-fixing story takes an interesting turn in 1999. In February, the Pakistan cricket team is touring India. We have just run a cover on how the team is emerging as a brand ambassador for its country—meeting kids and underprivileged people in India, and generally making a good name for itself. The cover after that is a sudden reversal. A source, a former Pakistan cricketer, flies to Delhi without much notice, meets me and hands over a dossier. The Justice Malik Muhammad Qayyum Commission of Inquiry, which has been looking into match-fixing in the Pakistan cricket team, had just submitted its report the previous month. The player hands me the entire report. Things cannot get more exciting.

On 3 January 1999, Wasim Akram was announced as captain until the World Cup, even though he featured prominently on the list of those accused of match-fixing, along with Salim Malik, Ijaz Ahmed, Mushtaq Ahmed, Waqar Younus, Inzamam-ul-Haq, Moin Khan, Akram Raza, Saqlain Mushtaq and Saeed Anwar.

This report is pure gold. For the February tour of India, the Pakistan Cricket Board initially wanted to keep five players away: Akram, Waqar, Ijaz, Moin Khan and Salim Malik. But it doesn't happen.

The long and detailed Qayyum inquiry opens not just a can but a barrel of worms. It is a huge exposé, and takes the Indian match-fixing story, which we broke in 1997, quite a few steps ahead. With access to this report, we have at our fingertips recorded statements of eminent cricketers like Javed Miandad, Majid Khan, Imran Khan, Saleem Pervez and Intikhab Alam during the inquiry. The commission has also found some players guilty, mentioning in detail certain incidents involving bookies and members of the team.

Javed Miandad, who coaches the team, has pointed squarely at the prevalent malpractices from his vantage as both coach and former player. He says Mushtaq Ahmed had confided to him that 'match-fixing is going on, and that once he was also involved ...' He reveals more, stating, 'In 1992-1993, when I was captain, I was informed by Idrees, brother of Hanif Kentbury (a bookmaker) that he had bought three of my players, Wasim Akram, Waqar Younus and another whose name I don't remember.'

Former cricketer Saleem Pervez also apparently confided in Miandad about paying 'Salim Malik, Mushtaq Ahmed, Inzamam and Waqar.' In his statement, Miandad says Pervez had stayed in the same hotel as the Pakistan team for a series, and if he claimed to have paid money to the players, it could well be true. Miandad also raises questions about Saeed Anwar's injury in an Australasia Cup match, and suggests that Pakistan's loss may have been orchestrated.

Former player and captain Imran Khan sings the same tune. Like Miandad, he insists that a fixed match cannot be the result of a single player's corrupt practices, and that a number of good players have to be involved to guarantee that the results go a certain way. He also corroborates Miandad's statement that there were rumours of players selling out to bookies, and that Miandad had called to inform him about it. He says, 'I believe match-fixing has taken place as players have made allegations, including the current captain ... Intikhab Alam ... is a decent person. If he has stated that there has been match-fixing, he should be believed.'

Intikhab Alam, the former manager of the team, clearly recounts multiple anonymous phone calls to his room alleging match-fixing against four or five of his top players. After a particularly dismal team performance, he had called the players to his room to enquire about the matter. It is at this time, he says, that Basit Ali 'confessed he was involved in match-fixing ... Waqar Younus and Salim Malik denied the allegation.' He also recounts how Asif Iqbal clearly told him that the bookies had lost forty lakh rupees and would occasionally call him to ask for information.

The Pakistan team's CEO, Majid Khan, also points out inconsistencies, with out-of-form batsmen being sent out higher in the batting order. He says that when he confronted the coach, Haroon Rashid, about these repeated mistakes, Rashid told him in frustration that 'if the captain was unwilling to win the match, what could the coach do?'

Aamer Sohail, the captain, alleges that despite being in top form, he is being consistently run out in crucial matches. Rashid Latif repeats his testimony that despite repeatedly swearing on the holy Quran, most players regularly met bookies and dealt with them. Aaqib Javed has had altercations with Ejaz Ahmed about the fact that bookies openly visited him in a hotel room.

All the players who testify say that they have been offered money, sometimes as much as fifty lakh rupees. Javed says he was offered fifty lakh and a Pajero by a bookmaker: 'I came to know some players had taken vehicles. At my persuasion, two of them returned them. One was Waqar Younus.'

Things get murkier when the middleman, Saleem Pervez, confesses that 'Mushtaq and Saleem Malik had received $100,000 from me on behalf of someone for fixing the match in Sri Lanka ... I handed over the dollars to both of them who were together in their hotel room. The two players had contacted me directly in this connection. They asked for a larger amount but I told them I had only $100,000.' Mark Waugh testifies that Salim Malik had tried for hours to persuade him to get involved in match-fixing. He says he complained to the management, but did not make a formal allegation.

Ironically, I have become very friendly with Shahryar Khan, the Pakistani team manager of the 1999 tour, and have rekindled my acquaintance with Wasim Akram. Shahryar is a former diplomat and belongs to the erstwhile royal family of Bhopal. Both Shahryar and Akram had helped arrange for their team to interact with disadvantaged kids and that was the focus of the *Outlook* cover story—the one that is succeeded by this very different cover, which embarrasses nearly all the members of the touring cricket team. The relationship between these team members and their coach, Javed Miandad, also turns frosty because of Miandad's statement to the Qayyum inquiry, which my story highlights.

## LANCE KLUSENER COMES TO *OUTLOOK*

Another cricketer who becomes very friendly with me during these years is the South African all-rounder Lance Klusener. We become particularly close during a golfing Pro Am event that he comes to play in Gurgaon, along with Desmond Haynes, Gordon Greenidge and others. On this trip, I take Klusener to the *Outlook* office in New Delhi, and he meets with Vinod and some others. Vinod presents him with a timepiece, with great fanfare, while the rest of us cringe with embarrassment. The timepiece is one of the gifts that the magazine gives out for three-year subscriptions.

2000 is a landmark year for cricket because of the breaking of the Hansie Cronje match-fixing story. Sometime earlier, in that same year, Mark Mascarenhas announces the launch of his cricket magazine *Cricket Talk*. He requests me to get Klusener and some of the other South African cricketers to the launch venue at the Oberoi Hotel in Bombay. Klusener and I are really pally, but he refuses to attend and will absolutely not budge. Neither do any of the other South African cricketers I know personally. I detect a great tension amongst them. Even the normally chirpy Herschelle Gibbs is silent.

Putting two and two together after the revelations, I surmise that the tension must have been between the different groups in the team. Some were resisting match-fixing, and some others had perhaps taken up Hansie's offer. That evening, only the captain accompanied me to the function. In the cab, he kept asking me questions about his own team members—who was talking with whom and what reasons they had given me for not coming. I think the players had come to know that Cronje was going to the function, and wanted to avoid meeting him. That's the reason they declined to come to the magazine's launch.

## *TEHELKA*: THE BUSINESS PLAN

I leave *Outlook* in 1999 to be part of the editorial team starting *Cricket Talk*. But this is the dot-com era, and I soon find myself harbouring ambitions to start an online investigative portal.

I zero in on the name 'Tehelka'. Sometime in the fall, I call my cousin Ashish Mehra in California and have him register the domain. You can't use your Indian credit card for overseas online transactions; it almost never goes through.

I also make a business plan and start approaching venture capitalists to pitch them my idea. I get some traction. I am doing all this in my free time as we are only ideating on *Cricket Talk* thus far. The launch is still many months away.

Sometime during this period, Tarun and I reconnect. He too is putting something together with adman Suhel Seth, and suggests we all team up. One fine day in February 2000, Tarun, Suhel, Minty

(Tarun's brother) and I take a flight to Bombay to pitch our idea to Ashok Wadhwa at Ambit. The cab ride from the airport with Tarun and Minty is an unforgettable one. Tarun's black humour wafts us along.

Wadhwa is a short, bearded man. He is the only person from Ambit in the conference room. Tarun gets up and pitches the idea of an online portal with investigations as a key ingredient. He uses the talking points that I have prepared for him, based on my own individual hunt for capital. I get up and speak for about two minutes—largely on how our content will also work as our advertising budget. In an industry where dot-coms are spending crores of capital on advertising, our stories will accomplish that job for us. Suhel too speaks along these lines—it is an idea whose time has come.

Wadhwa listens attentively throughout our pitch. He asks a few questions. When all is over, he gets up and ruminates silently. Then be picks up a piece of chalk and writes the figure '8' on the board.

We look at each other. What the fuck does it mean? Suhel seems to be the only person who understands this secret code.

'Boss, he is giving a valuation to our idea at eight million dollars,' whispers Suhel.

Then Wadhwa goes on to explain how he will raise the first one million dollars for us. We are enthralled. The dollar is just a little over forty rupees.

We leave Wadhwa's office in a trance. Suhel gives us a burst of his Neanderthal laughter and takes the route leading straight to Hotel President so we can digest what has just happened. There, in the coffee shop, he freezes the equity that each of us owns by writing it on a paper table mat. Luckily, I preserve it as a souvenir, for later it will become part of the evidence at the Justice Venkataswami Commission of Inquiry, to debunk the government's falsehoods about the origin of *Tehelka*.

From the President, Tarun, Minty and I head for a meeting with Shankar Sharma of First Global to discuss the Ambit valuation, as we want to understand more about the venture-funding process and also check on the robustness of the valuation. Shankar is an old friend of Minty and Tarun.

After we come back to Delhi from Bombay, I resign from *Cricket Talk*. It all happens rather quickly. Mark calls me, and sensing there's something afoot from the way I speak, keeps prodding me till I tell him that I am leaving for a start-up. He gets really upset.

Tarun, by then, has already resigned from *Outlook*, though he is still serving out his notice period. I start getting nervous after my resignation. Although Ambit has picked up the mandate of getting us the seed money at a valuation of US$ 8 million, we don't have any sense of a time frame within which this might happen.

A few other things happen within a week of this. Wadhwa visits Delhi and meets Tarun. When Tarun broaches the subject of a bridge loan till such time as the seeding round is placed, Wadhwa's response is noncommittal. At that point, we are already ideating and making possible employee lists, and this dampens our enthusiasm a bit. Though Suhel offers his advertising agency offices to us to start functioning, Tarun doesn't much like the idea for a variety of reasons. Shankar Sharma then lands up in Delhi on a personal visit and meets Tarun, and it turns out that he wants to invest in our start-up too, at the same valuation. That changes the nature of the game. We are infinitely more comfortable dealing with a venture capitalist who is also a friend and willing to start us on our way immediately than someone who is just a venture capitalist and isn't giving us any time frame for capital infusion. So we decide to switch the mandate to First Global and inform Wadhwa of our decision.

# BOARD MEETINGS AT *TEHELKA*

While First Global starts giving us the seed money in tranches, our burn rate in just a few months shoots up to between Rs 30 lakh and Rs 40 lakh. So we are also in constant conversation with venture capitalists for our second round of funding. Our initiative is shaping up to be ahead of its time. As our traffic grows, we start getting ranked highly by Alexa, the online traffic statistic company. We begin to produce multimedia content, sometimes even venturing into entertainment. For instance, we produce a TV series for Zee TV. Our multimedia team is headed by Minty Tejpal and has great talent—Amrish Sethi, Munna and others. We also produce content for foundations. So a big part of our revenue stream is based on diverse content generation. For a while, Rahul Johry, who will later gain fame as the CEO of BCCI, works for us and puts together several content partnerships for us.

In many ways, since *Tehelka* is the first serious news platform being set up by established journalists, there is a great deal of interest around it. In several interviews, we assert that mainline journalism has become much too soft, and we aim to bring back hard and combative journalism, adversarial to power and completely aligned with public interest. Tarun says, 'Most media companies are now led by the commercial impulse, *Tehelka* will try and be led by the editorial impulse.'

The team that is quickly assembled is a fine mix of experience and raw talent, of talented writers and hard-bitten reporters, and it is capable of the widest coverage.

Within a few months of starting up, *Tehelka* establishes a reputation for excellent reviews of arts and culture, as well as political and social analysis. The attempt is to try and break new ground in every area and to exploit the innate elasticity of the medium to do long-form interviews and stories (as is seldom possible in traditional journalism). Our tagline—'News. Views. All the juice.'—sums up the ambition. In no time, a terrific array of Indian writers in English—both established and upcoming—from across the world begin to write regularly for the site. Among the writers regularly contributing to *Tehelka* are Amitava Kumar, Dom Moraes, Farrukh Dhondy, Kiran Nagarkar and Manjula Padmanabhan. Dom Moraes becomes a regular visitor to our office along with his wife, Sarayu.

As part of the attempt to push the envelope, *Tehelka* pioneers a highly candid sex and relationships channel, which showcases not just reportage but also original erotic fiction. In all this, the journalistic principle, as enunciated in the beginning, of maximising ground reportage—hard stories—is kept at the forefront.

Soon, *Tehelka* is putting up fifteen–twenty new stories every single day and getting reader responses and editorial contributions from across the world. Apart from the rich editorial fare, it also gets attention for the aesthetics of its design and its clever illustrations. A bunch of terrific young designers from the National Institute of Design work on gleaming, just-launched transparent Macs, churning out a superb array of artworks and graphics for the site every day. The look and feel of the site can stand favourable comparison with any contemporary news site.

In its first avatar, which lasts all of one year, *Tehelka* generates an excitement that is rare and unprecedented. Curiously, there is also a certain mystique attached to the venture. Perhaps because no one quite knows how this incredible new medium will handle traditional journalism.

Other ancillary factors also play into this—one being the composition of the *Tehelka* board of directors. The original board has three external directors. In order of age, if not eminence, they are Khushwant Singh, V.S. Naipaul and Amitabh Bachchan. In the first—and last—board meeting *Tehelka* is destined to hold, all three show up at our Soami Nagar office in September 2000. When Bachchan steps onto the edit floor unannounced, the entire team of journalists spontaneously stands up—so powerful is his aura in those days before the endless exposure of TV and Twitter. Soon after, Khushwant Singh, eighty-five years old but undaunted, climbs up slowly to the second floor to Tarun's office, where the meeting is being held. And Naipaul's presence, of course, has a mythic air, so seldom is he seen in India.

Memorably, the first thing Khushwant says to Bachchan when he walks in is, 'How's papa? It's been a long time since I met him.' In that relaxed, convivial mood, among other things, Bachchan spends ten minutes explaining to Khushwant how the internet and the *Tehelka* website work, and how this is going to be the future of global communications. Naipaul gives a short note on the virtues of good writing to the editors and journalists; an unexpected class from a modern master. Its contents will later be reproduced in books.

There is another oddball piece unfurling alongside. Given the very open journalistic and creative energy at *Tehelka*, Minty had one day shown up with a young, intense Sikh boy carrying a guitar, and asked him to play us a song. The Sufi number the boy sang was riveting. Minty wanted us to back his debut album, and with cavalier excitement, we decided to. Now, at the meeting, we give an update on our plans to the board, and the two songs the young Sikh has recorded are played. Bachchan loves them, and asks for a copy. *Tehelka* backs the creation of that album—with its scarce resources—and it goes on to become a pop phenomenon. The artiste is Rabbi Shergill. But given the storms *Tehelka* is to run into and the ways in which our collective and individual lives will be destroyed, none of us will ever make a single rupee from the album's massive success.

## FALLEN HEROES

Our first splashy story in *Tehelka* is 'Fallen Heroes'. It is an undercover documentary on match-fixing in Indian cricket. Manoj Prabhakar, for the first time, names the Indian teammate who offered him Rs 25 lakh to play below par against Pakistan in the 1994 Singer Cup in Sri Lanka. The name he discloses, understandably, creates a big furore in India: Kapil Dev. A preliminary inquiry has already been started by the CBI with regard to match-fixing, and summons arrive for Prabhakar to appear before the agency even while he is undercover, shooting his investigative documentary in collaboration with *Tehelka*.

The documentary's focus is on layering Prabhakar's story, bringing it together with the versions of those whom he said he had informed about the offer and, of course, other allied material. Among the people that Prabhakar said he had informed right then are Ravi Shastri, Sunil Gavaskar and Ajit Wadekar. It becomes Prabhakar's mission to get them talking about the 1994 incident. It would have required too much foresight on his part to have informed his teammates of a match-fixing offer in 1994 with the objective of using them as alibi several years later. It is with this in mind that he interacts with his former teammates.

Incidentally, I know both Gavaskar and Shastri well. I grew close to Shastri because of Mark, and spent time with him during the tour of New Zealand in 1998-1999 and the World Cup in the UK in 1999. So when Prabhakar decides to go pay his former teammates a visit, I am in a bit of a quandary. This doesn't last long as I can't in good faith deflect or discourage him from a legitimate journalistic pursuit.

Just about a year earlier, I had done a profile on Sunny Gavaskar, when he turned fifty. Sunny had opened up to me in a manner that was rare for him, and had given me several hours at his flat in Worli in Bombay. I quote verbatim from my piece:

> There was fun too in the breaking in of new players. One such pair was Maninder Singh and Laxman Sivaramakrishnan in the '82 tour to Pakistan when, freshly arrived at Karachi, Sunny took them to dinner to explain 'what playing for India was all about' and 'what was expected'. Both were in their mid-teens and after Sunny finished his pep talk, both went silent as death. Laughs Sunny, 'After a while I started getting nervous. They had absolutely nothing to say.' These two, along with Manoj Prabhakar and Kiran More, held a soft corner in Sunny's heart because of their attitude to the game.

Sunny had then mentioned Prabhakar to me as someone he admired for his attitude. But in Prabhakar's own interaction with him, he is too diplomatic to confirm what Prabhakar had confided to him during the 1994 Singer series, when Sunny was a commentator. After the story breaks, Sunny is never the same again with Prabhakar or me. He considers my part in it a personal betrayal for having 'allowed' Prabhakar to interact with him without as much as a hint about his motives. It is the same with Shastri. To his credit, Shastri comes out shining in his interaction with Prabhakar in his own inimitable, colourful way. He is honest enough to confirm that Prabhakar had indeed told him about the offer, and his wife Ritu reveals her suspicions about some other former players. In 2003, during the World Cup in South Africa, Ritu tears into me, at a cricketers' evening get-together, over the Fallen Heroes investigation. I keep silent.

The story gets *Tehelka* a lot of visibility and traffic. A piece of coverage that attracts my attention, in particular, is a screeching *Midday* headline in Bombay: the front page just says 'TEHELKA' in all caps. In an atmosphere where heavily funded digital platforms are spending millions on advertising, we are creating space just by the strength of our content. We are soon employing more than forty people, most of them journalists.

## THE LEAD-UP TO OPERATION WEST END

In the initial years at *Tehelka*, I spend some of my time building strategies to attract venture capitalists, along with Tarun, who, as a director, is thinking of possible revenue sources. But I am the head of the Tehelka Investigative Team, and the bulk of my time is consumed by our ongoing investigations. Working with me are Mathew Samuel, Sashi Kumar and Kumar Baadal.

After the fire in the Bharatpur ammunition depot at the end of April 2000 and the rumours associated with that fire, I start toying with the idea of exposing the underbelly of defence procurement in India. Mathew Samuel gets a good starting point to build an investigation along these lines, and we gradually work our way upwards. We plan an undercover investigation with Samuel posing as a liaison officer of West End International, a UK company allegedly involved in the manufacturing of high-end thermal binoculars suitable for the military. We develop bogus catalogues and a set of capabilities for our fictitious product and start working our way through the procurement process, meeting the concerned defence officials, army officers, bureaucrats, defence middlemen, politicians and so on, who can help us get our product trialled and evaluated by the Indian Army. We interact with several high-ranking army officers, defence middlemen and politicians like Bangaru Laxman, the president of the BJP, Jaya Jaitley and R.K. Jain, the president and treasurer respectively of the Samata Party, as well as others. The crucial meeting regarding our fictitious product takes place between Jaya Jaitely and Samuel at the residence of then defence minister George Fernandes.

My undercover appearances are limited as my face is relatively well known because of the interviews I have been giving on match-fixing. I clip my hair, wear spectacles, and give myself a so-called foreign accent to avoid being recognised. Samuel is just perfect for his undercover role. He has street instincts, is pot-bellied, and fits the image of a middleman. He is also dexterous enough to avoid generating too much suspicion.

We have to be conscious of battery time, expected tape duration and the danger levels of any particular location. Very often, there is a lot of waiting to be done before meetings start, and it would be disastrous if some particularly important chunk of conversation does not get recorded because the battery or the tape has run out.

We end up dishing out upwards of Rs 10 lakh to various people in the process of getting our product approved for trial and valuation by the Indian Army. Of course, we can't get any further. We don't actually have thermal binoculars which we can submit for trial and valuation!

It takes us around eight months, starting sometime in the month of August 2000, to get ready to break the investigation. Though our field work stops sometime in January 2001, it takes us a couple more months to complete the transcription of the tapes, write the script and edit the footage. Nearly a dozen journalists are involved in the transcription and production processes. We have approximately hundred hours of footage that we cull into a four-and-a-half-hour-long documentary called Operation West End.

When we enter the production phase, the machines take a lot of time to render the video. They run all night and day, and sometimes they crash, leading to considerable stress. There is also the tension of keeping things under wraps. The whole production unit is more or less hermetically sealed. I want no one to know more than they are supposed to. So, those transcribing the tapes don't know which characters figure in the tapes their colleagues are transcribing. Nobody walking the corridors of our office can glance at a computer screen to see what is being edited. Voice-overs have to be done at night when few people are around.

I spend close to sixteen hours everyday in office, overseeing things. We make duplicates of the original tapes and keep one set in bank lockers for fear that a set could get destroyed or stolen. I tell myself that I will never put myself through such a grind for any story again. Little do I know what a blazing cauldron we are about to fall into.

## OPERATION WEST END: THE GOOF-UPS

When we break Operation West End on 13 March 2001, all hell breaks loose. Though we wrap up our story about selling non-existent thermal imagers to the Indian Army successfully, there are many close calls during the investigation. Once, Mathew Samuel is on his way to a meeting in a rickshaw, right in the middle of his exalted undercover role of a moneyed liaison officer. When his rickshaw stops at a red light, next to it stops a Mercedes. In the back seat is the middleman he is to meet in the office nearby. It is winter, so Samuel quickly pulls his jacket over his face and hopes the guy hasn't noticed.

Another time, a colonel gets very suspicious and insists on seeing what is inside Samuel's briefcase. This is the briefcase which contains the cameras and all the recording equipment. One of the cameras is activated when the briefcase is stood vertically and the other when it is placed horizontally. Samuel is forced to make an excuse and exit the location.

For the meeting with Jaya Jaitley at George Fernandes's residence, Samuel is armed with two cameras. One is the contraption in the briefcase, and the other is a camera in a tie device. The recorder in the tie device has to be strapped on Samuel's back, and the device is huge compared to future models. It can be switched on and off with a vibrator switch. When on, it keeps vibrating to indicate that the device is recording. The vibrator is buzzing safely in Samuel's pocket when he starts the meeting, but at some point, it slips from his pocket to inside his underpants. He has to live with that sensation through the duration of the meeting.

In his undercover role as the chief liaison officer of West End International, Samuel also commits a series of goof-ups that should have given the game away but don't.

Below, I excerpt from a piece I wrote around that time. TiT stands for Tehelka Investigative Team:

> I will here narrate a few incidents of the kind of tomfoolery that should have blown our cover much earlier than it did.
>
> At a meeting with General Murgai (retired), who was serving when we first met him, he asked a TiT member the range of our thermal imaging cameras. With characteristic sincerity, promptness and pomp, our member replied, 'Unlimited.' Observing the bewildered expression on the general's face, he tried to retrieve the situation: 'No, no, what I meant is that after a long distance the vision gets blurred.'
>
> At another meeting with Murgai, he asked who the bankers were for West End. Our illustrious TiT member said, 'Thomas Cook.'

Don't laugh yet. I will just reproduce the conversation:

Murgai: Achcha, tumhare udhar West End ke voh...who are your bankers in West End?

T: Hain?

Murgai: In West End International, who are the bankers?

T: Thomas Cook.

Murgai: Haan?

T: Thomas Cook.

Murgai: Thomas Cook. Because you see, the balance … when will you give?

Here's one more. The coup de grâce. Mohinder Singh Sahni, the honorary consular general of Belize and a defence middleman, asks the same TiT member where he stays in England. His answer: 'Manchester United'!

## HOLI ACRIMONY

There is tremendous pressure on the team in the run-up to D-day. We had initially planned on a release later in the month, but have a strong suspicion that our cover has been blown, and hence the rush to advance the story.

There are no holidays for us during the production phase. Not even on Holi, which falls about a week before the release. But we have a delayed start on Holi day—we decide to start at five in the evening, after all the revelries are over.

So, at around five, I reach Tarun's house to collect the keys to the office, which is a hundred yards from his home. The Holi party is in full swing at his place. The guests are all colourful and drunk, and try to plaster me with colours as I wait for the keys. While most of them back off after being firmly rebuffed, there is one friend who is persistent and won't take my refusal at face value. He colours my face good and proper. I lose it completely and lash out at him. It creates quite a furore, and several people have to intervene.

I think my reaction is a result of the immense stress—by Holi, I am overcome with paranoia. I am paranoid that the production process might go off the rails. Paranoid that those we are exposing will come to know of our real identities and organise a legal manoeuvre of some kind. Paranoid that somebody will leak information, not out of malice but by simple bragging. I apologise to the friend later, when I bump into him at an airport, but the incident has soured our friendship.

When the story breaks and people come to know what we have been working on, they understand the extent of stress I was under. I am not *just* a crazed Allahabadi anymore.

## THE *TEHELKA* WITCH-HUNT

India has never been a safe haven for whistleblowers. We have always been a country where the levers of power are more amenable to be used for the pursuit of political vendettas, be it against politicians or the media or activists.

When *Tehelka* first breaks Operation West End on 13 March 2001, no BJP spokesperson appears on national television for a full two days. The party is probably stunned to see images of its president, Bangaru Laxman, taking bundles of cash to help promote a defence product. That the country's defence procurement system is so porous that journalists could run amok by posing as sales representatives of a patently fictitious product speaks a lot about the checks and balances within the system and the greed that envelops it. That they could have a meeting at the residence of the defence minister is the icing on the cake and revelatory of the state of the nation. For the first time in independent India, people see visual images of corruption at play, and the impact on society at large is deep and lasting.

Initial reports indicate that Prime Minister Atal Behari Vajpayee is depressed by the magnitude of the *Tehelka* story and considering resigning, to the consternation of his colleagues in the cabinet, but the mood soon passes. The baton is passed to the likes of National Security Advisor Brajesh Mishra, law minister Arun Jaitely and George Fernandes, to teach *Tehelka* a lesson.

You cannot really plan for an assault by the state. For nearly thirty months after Operation West End, the Indian government wages a pitched battle of perception in the media, based on false and vicious allegations and conjectures about *Tehelka*. The attempted smearing has the clear objective of creating doubts about the website's credentials in the minds of the public, in order to exonerate the guilty and blunt the impact of the revelations.

George Fernandes, the defence minister, who resigns after the story breaks but is re-instituted by Prime Minister Vajpayee, variously accuses Operation West End of being an ISI plot, an Opposition plot, a plot engineered by 'middlemen who had lost their access to the defence ministry consequent upon decisions (he had) taken', and a story backed by the Hinduja group. Various NDA leaders allege similar conspiracies, going so far as to claim that the *Tehelka* investigation is a massive stock-market conspiracy engineered by 'anti-nationals' for private gain, with the intention of destabilising the country.

Within a few days of West End breaking, a campaign of misinformation is started on this count by different arms of the government against *Tehelka*'s first-round investor, First Global.

Let me give you a flavour of the NDA's assault on First Global for the simple act of investing in *Tehelka*. In the first ten years of its life, First Global had virtually no worries about tax or legal infringement. In fact, it paid more in taxes in 2000 than companies like Proctor & Gamble, Ranbaxy, Titan and Raymonds. However, after Operation West End, First Global is served over two hundred summons and raided twenty-five times. Shankar Sharma and Devina Mehra, promoters of First Global, are twice physically detained; seventeen of their offices are shut; their properties are attacked. They are banned from trading and forbidden to travel overseas on the specious count that they *might* evade a tax liability that *might* come up at some future date. Their accounts are frozen without even a chargesheet under the Reserve Bank of India's wide-reaching powers to issue 'any directives' to banks. Their laptops are seized, and Shankar is arrested and kept behind bars for more than ten weeks under a law that was repealed eighteen months prior by Parliament, precisely because it was draconian and prone to this kind of misuse.

Of course, nearly everyone who is exposed by the West End investigation claims that the tapes are doctored. Jaya Jaitley is one of the most vocal. It is only after almost a year of insisting that the tapes are doctored and denying that she has ever met anyone or accepted anything, as shown in the *Tehelka* tapes, that she will finally admit that the meeting did indeed take place in her room in the defence minister's house and a packet changed hands. Her excuse? She thought it contained sweets!

The Vajpayee government announces the Justice Venkataswami Commission of Inquiry on 24 March 2001. It would have been a welcome initiative except that the government reveals a sinister intent in the commission's mandate. Term D in the commission's terms of reference authorises it to look into 'all aspects relating to the making and publication of these allegations'.

Term D is unprecedented in the history of commissions in India. It allows the Centre to shift the focus from the message to the messenger. Arun Jaitley's brainchild proves to be the most effective means of media harassment that any government can implement. A.G. Noorani argues precisely this in an editorial in the *Hindustan Times* dated 31 March 2001:

> Never in the half century of the Commission of Inquiry Act, 1952 was the body ever asked to probe into the credentials of those who had made the charges. The focus was on the message, never the messenger. If this move is allowed to pass muster, the press will be effectively muzzled. Any time it publishes an exposé, the government will retaliate by setting up inquiries not only into the truth of the charges, but also the motives, finances and sources of the journal which published them. It is not only invidious to single out the press for discriminatory treatment, it is also unconstitutional to do so.

Many of the accused also cast doubts on the transcripts prepared by *Tehelka* for the tapes. So the commission orders the tapes to be re-transcribed by the Government of India. The Vigyan Bhavan annexe, where the proceedings are taking place, now witnesses the spectacle of government employees transcribing tapes. While the *Tehelka* transcripts had about a dozen or so errors (in a wordage of about half a million), the transcription by the Government of India employees turns out to be quite a mess. The Justice Venkataswami Commission rules twice that the tapes are genuine. Later, even the CBI will conduct forensic tests and find that the tapes are kosher.

The government does not file a single affidavit against anyone who has been incriminated by our exposé. Yet it files hundreds of pages of concocted theories, accusations and outright lies on sworn affidavits. The full venality of the approach can be understood if one examines the affidavits. The accusations are either outright lies or leaps of imagination, or flanked by phrases like 'presumably', 'further investigation is still on', 'deducing from this', and 'obviously Tehelka was'.

The Government of India fails to issue a single summons against anyone incriminated by the *Tehelka* investigation. It does not cross-examine even one accused person on the stand. However, Tarun Tejpal is cross-examined for a full four days by no less a person than the additional solicitor general, Kirit Rawal. The questions range from how many cars he owns, how many office computers there are in the offices of *Tehelka*, to whether he was late in filing his income tax returns seven years ago! Then, Mathew Samuel and I are grilled for a month each by forty lawyers. Each and every aspect of the tapes is examined. New meanings and motives are superimposed on situations where none exist.

From 2005 onwards, it will be the CBI that launches prosecutions against all the accused figuring on the *Tehelka* tapes, which will subsequently lead to the conviction of BJP president Bangaru Laxman in 2012 and Jaya Jaitley in 2020. Vindication will come, ultimately, but at a great cost to the media platform and the journalists concerned.

## THE CBI RAID

We are preparing for the cross-examination of Jaya Jaitley at the Justice Venkataswami Commission of Inquiry. Ostensibly set up to look into the various revelations made by Operation West End, it has degenerated into a witch-hunt against *Tehelka*, led by senior judicial officers, both within and outside the commission. They are suitably aided by several wings of the government, notably the

CBI, the Enforcement Directorate, the Income Tax Department, and even the Delhi Police.

Most people in the office are groggy from lack of sleep, as we have been busy preparing with our lawyers for Jaitley's cross-questioning. As we get ready to leave around nine in the morning, a fleet of cars screeches to a stop outside our office in Soami Nagar in south Delhi.

Out troop about ten CBI officers with great zest and energy, the majority of them in safari suits. Leading them is a senior of mine from school. He is chewing paan, or maybe not. I don't remember clearly.

'*Arrey sir, aap,*' I exclaim. '*Itne action mein.*' Oh, sir, it's you. In action, no less.

Maybe he spits out some paan at this point. Maybe not.

'Arrey, what to do, I kept telling the CBI director that I know Aniruddha. He's from my school. But he said it's okay—go conduct the raid. So I agreed. But it was clear to him that I know you,' he says.

The raid is ostensibly to dig out proof to substantiate a poaching charge the CBI has fabricated against one of our reporters, Kumar Baadal. The case is still meandering through the UP courts.

## UP CLOSE AND PERSONAL WITH THE LAW

After everybody else has given their testimony in the West End inquiry, it is the turn of the *Tehelka* journalists. I am personally cross-examined by three dozen lawyers for nearly a month. It is an exhausting experience. Though the story is relatively fresh in my head, the pitfalls of memory are soon evident. It's tough to remember things sequentially, or even facts the right way around, at the best of times. And here the lawyers are, actively trying to pick holes in your story—the particular voice-overs you wrote, where you stored the tapes, who said what and when, and so on.

While we were undercover with West End, the story had grown in value incrementally. It was anybody's guess as to where it would all end. We never kept a daily diary or anything at all to register facts in an organised way. The tapes were the ultimate evidence. I had scribbled notes on my copy of the script, marking where to go looking for particular bits of the transcript, and this works well for me during the cross-examination. However, when I start relying on my notes during re-examination, there's a big hue and cry. It seems I am expected to remember hundred hours of transcripts without any aid at all.

There are many heated exchanges with the opposing lawyers. Once, I have a big tiff with Kirit Rawal, the additional solicitor general of India, when he starts casting aspersions on the royalties I have got for *Bunker 13*, and the two of us have a go at each other. I also remember a big shouting match between the solicitor general of India, Harish Salve, and Prashant Bhushan. I have never seen Prashant so angry.

Two lawyers from the other side are particularly impressive. One is Niloy Datta, who is the counsel for Jaya Jaitley, and the other is N. Hariharan, who represents P. Sashi, the starting point of our investigation in many ways.

The case affords us the privilege of working with some great senior lawyers. I end up briefing the likes of Shanti Bhushan, Ram Jethmalani, Kapil Sibal, Rajeev Dhavan, Dushyant Dave and a host of other seniors, and have the opportunity to observe their work ethics from up close. It is scary how they manage their time. Once, I have to brief Jethmalani on an issue, but he has no time to spare the day before my hearing, so he calls me at six in the morning on the day of the hearing and understands my brief as he goes about his early morning routine.

The two lawyers who give us the most time to be fully prepared before a hearing are Shanti Bhushan and Jethmalani. They are a cut above the others in terms of the hard work they put in. Jethmalani's cross-examination of the government witnesses is brilliant. He toys with them and makes the income tax officers admit to details that make Harish Salve and Rawal so nervous that they stop the inquiry into the financial 'conspiracy' behind West End then and there. They just take their witnesses off the stands and say they don't want to pursue the matter anymore. This is a huge victory for us. All thanks to Ram uncle, as we call him.

The lawyers who take us through on a day-to-day basis are Kevin Gulati, Siddharth Luthra, Pramod Dubey and Midhanshu Tripathi. The amount of time they spend at the commission, giving up their daily practice, is mind blowing. All of them do it pro bono. For Kevin, my classmate from Allahabad, it is a great learning experience. He probably gains a lot of confidence after going up against the best in the business in a David vs Goliath situation. He even does a few cross-examinations, though he does not have a background in criminal law. A few of these are so good that Hariharan advises him to start a criminal practice!

For Luthra, there is an emotional aspect at play. He ends up cross-examining George Fernandes on behalf of *Tehelka*. Ironically, during the Emergency era, his father, the eminent K.K. Luthra, had defended Fernandes from Indira Gandhi's regime. Aiding Siddharth Luthra in his various cross-examinations and strategies is his junior, Pramod Dubey, who provides insights into statements and affidavits that you never would have thought possible.

The other motivating factor that keeps our defence functioning is the energy of Rani Jethmalani. She has legal preparatory sessions at her father's place, and all the junior lawyers and *Tehelka* staffers are fed lavishly. Prashant Bhushan is always there with his unflappable presence and steady moral compass. Never fazed by any situation, he is like a rock to us.

Another senior lawyer, Gopal Subramanium, who happens to be the commission's own counsel along with Sidharth Agarwal and Rajshekhar Rao, maintains a vigorous impartiality in the face of a very determined Union of India, which has every intention of twisting the knife in us by hook or by crook. In fact, it is rumoured that the BJP leaders have offered Subramanium a Supreme Court justiceship at a very young age if he does their bidding in the commission. That he doesn't bend to them is a tribute, not only to him, but to a legal system which, at this point, is capable of producing people like him.

Though Kapil Sibal never appears for us at the commission, he does constantly advise us on legal issues that emanate for us from the commission and other cases. In court craft, Sibal is in a league of his own, and his ability to distil an issue to its finest point is unique. He is also not your typical defence lawyer. These days, lawyers like to please the judges too much. He is not one of those. On top of that, he is very public spirited and does several cases pro bono. Dushyant Dave is another brave soul. He calls a case the way it is, on the points of law. He is never intimidated by the judge or by the lawyers on the other side.

Looking back on those years, I must say again, as I have said a thousand times, that if it had not been for the many lawyers who stood up for us pro bono, it would have been virtually impossible for us to survive that period.

Sometime in November 2002, Justice Venkataswami resigns from the commission because the Congress criticises him in Parliament for becoming the chairman of the authority on advance ruling on customs and excise. I hear lawyers from the government, especially Rawal, croak about how the Congress has scored a self-goal, presumably because they weren't getting their way with the judge. We always felt that he ruled fairly. With his going, the government appoints former Supreme Court justice Sailendu Nath Phukan as the head of the commission. We take the decision to boycott the commission, as the new judge never gives us the assurance of fair practice that we expect from the system. In 2004, after the UPA comes to power, they rescind the commission, and the inquiry becomes infructuous. Shortly thereafter, the government passes on the investigation into the tapes to the CBI, and it initiates several prosecutions that are still making their way through the judicial system.

But it also creates a situation where Mathew Samuel, Tarun and I become star witnesses for the CBI in the *Tehelka*-Operation West End cases it is prosecuting but the main accused in the Official Secrets Act that the CBI launches against us.

## THE OFFICIAL SECRETS ACT

On 31 March 2001, eighteen days after Operation West End, the CBI is used to register an FIR against *Tehelka* using the Official Secrets Act. This has to do with a story allegedly published on the *Tehelka* website in October 2000. We later learn of the sequence of events that led up to this.

It turns out that, on 20 March 2001, someone called up George Fernandes's office at his residence and asked to speak to him. The caller identified himself as Harish Chandra Prasad, a contractor with the Railways, and said that he had urgent information to share on the 'conspiracy' behind the *Tehelka* investigation. He also claimed that he was a socialist. After a few minutes of pause and reflection, the office called Prasad back and asked him to come for a meeting with Fernandes, at midnight, at his residence.

Prasad sold to Fernandes the theory that a conspiracy had been hatched in the chamber of a director of the Ministry of Home Affairs (MHA), Thomas Mathew. Apparently, Mathew and his cohorts felt that Fernandes was 'saffronising' socialism, and wanted to bring him down. Fernandes was shown visitors' passes at North Block as evidence of Prasad's meeting with Thomas Mathew. The next day, Fernandes called up a newspaper. A front page report was published on 22 March 2001 by the *Pioneer*, under the headline 'Conspiracy Unravels: Govt official mentor of Tehelka Sting.'

The very next day, the MHA, citing the *Pioneer* news item, prepared a long list of charges, seeking clarifications from Thomas Mathew. Some of these charges were ludicrous. Para 1.4 of the show cause notice was plain absurd:

> Whether the statement attributed to him (Shri Thomas Mathew) in the news item that 'he was working to bring down the Government and that he did not mind using the ISI, Naxals and insurgents' is correct?

The government's line of vendetta was made explicit. Certain newspapers linked Thomas Mathew with Christian missionaries and insurgent groups in the Northeast, and also tried to bring Vishnu Bhagwat, a former admiral of the India Navy, who had been sacked from his post, into the grand conspiracy theory. On 30 March 2001, the *Hindustan Times* published a lead story on its front page: 'CBI has nothing on "fall guy": New Turn in Tehelka aftermath leaves Govt flummoxed.' The newspaper claimed that the CBI had conveyed to the home ministry that no conclusive evidence had been uncovered of Mathew's involvement with organisations engaged in subversive activities.

The name of another junior officer, Niraj Kumar, was then brought into the picture. Kumar was working in the North East Division of the home ministry as a section officer in the year 1999. He got married in December 2000. The government suspended him after three days of his getting married, merely on grounds of contemplation of disciplinary proceedings. He was not served a show cause notice or given any reason for this abrupt action by the government.

It was easier to build a narrative around Kumar, as he was a mere section officer. Home Minister L.K. Advani himself went to great lengths to put the blame on Kumar for the *Tehelka* investigation, in an interview to AajTak on 26 March 2001. Following the interview, agency sleuths visited Munikra, in south Delhi, where Kumar once lived, and picked up different men called Niraj Kumar from the locality. These men showed utter ignorance about the *Tehelka* portal and the alleged conspiracy. It was then discovered that the MHA had furnished an old address for Kumar.

On 30 March 2001, the MHA filed a formal complaint with the CBI to investigate the alleged leak of certain documents from the North East Division of the home ministry. These documents had allegedly been published on the *Tehelka* portal in October 2000. The CBI registered an FIR on the same day against Niraj Kumar and unknown persons under Sections 3 and 5 of the draconian Official Secrets Act, 1923.

And so we find ourselves embroiled in a new legal struggle. The filing of an FIR over an old and insignificant issue is clearly an attempt to put *Tehelka* in its place and teach a lesson to a media platform that has pushed the government into a corner.

The unknown persons turn out to be Mathew Samuel, Tarun Tejpal and I. Subsequently, the CBI calls Tarun and me several times for questioning. In November 2005, I get bail in the case.

MHA director Thomas Mathew and Mathew Samuel are eventually granted bail too. In the meantime, the court issues summons to Tarun and Minty Tejpal, as they are the directors of Buffalo Network Pvt. Ltd, Tehelka's parent company.

The case meanders through several courts in Tees Hazari, and it takes eleven years before even the argument on framing of charges can begin. The whole thing is Kafqaesque—the Government of India is prosecuting four journalists and two officers of the MHA for an article that allegedly appeared on the *Tehelka* website and which apparently stated, quoting home ministry memos, that the Government of India was concerned about the work of Dutch NGOs in the Northeast! It would have been comic if it weren't for the fact that a conviction under the Official Secrets Act, a British-era relic that should have been scrapped after Independence, carries with it a stiff prison sentence.

In 2012, charges are framed on the grounds that the disclosure of the minutes of a meeting on the activities of foreign NGOs constitutes a crime since it affects the friendly relations of the country with foreign states. During the argument, it is hotly argued that the government needs to define a 'friendly' state, since the Netherlands and several western countries had imposed sanctions on India during the post-Pokhran nuclear test phase, and these had not been lifted at the time of the alleged publication.

In fact, documents are placed on record on behalf of Niraj Kumar that the Union of India had stated in Parliament—in reply to Parliament Question Number 46 (Lok Sabha), dated 17 July 2002, and submitted by two parliamentarians, Nawal Kishore Rai and Sushil Kumar Indora—that India was concerned over the presence of terrorist or secessionist organisations like NSCN (I-Muivah), Babbar Khalsa International, Hizbullah and the LTTE in the Netherlands. The government also said that it was taking up the matter with the kingdom of the Netherlands on a regular basis, and urging them to exercise caution in granting refugee status to these persons and to take precautions so that these organisations did not use the soil of the Netherlands to work against India.

Such is the confusion in court that in reply to the application moved for discharge, the CBI categorically states that the article published on the *Tehelka* website was opposed to the 'rule' of America. A small typographical error, 'o' becoming 'u', completely changes the context and makes for some humour in court.

You had to be there to believe the farcical nature of these hearings. Each judge had to be educated afresh about the matter. In 2007, when the case had reached a special CBI judge, he repeatedly asked the prosecution to provide the geographical location of the Netherlands, as, according to the prosecution, it was the main aggrieved party in the case. The prosecution obviously had not come armed with an atlas or globe and said that they would be unable to throw light on the location of the country in that particular hearing. The judge then asked the prosecution why *Tehelka* had a 'chilli' in its logo. The prosecution had no satisfactory answer. After that, there was a lot of brouhaha about the Netherlands and the *Tehelka* chilli. The judge was visibly exasperated and started dictating his order sheet for the day. In this, he mentioned NGOs from Finland instead of the Netherlands as being involved in financial activities in India. When one of the accused butted in to correct him, the judge blew up. 'You think you are the only intelligent person in the world,' he yelled. By this time, we were all struggling to keep a straight face. Finally, the judge decided not to record anything at all in the order sheet as the confusion between the Netherlands, Finland and the *Tehelka* chilli remained unresolved. Later, this judge was elevated to the position of justice in a high court, and he remained in service till recently.

Almost every hearing is farcical, and it is also a lot of time going down the drain. Over eleven years, there must have been at least a hundred hearings, if not more. The CBI never loses steam or energy while pushing the case.

Sometime in 2012-2013, I move the Delhi High Court for quashing of the chargesheet. With elections coming up in 2014, I can't stop worrying about the ominous turn the case might take if the BJP comes to power. So I go and pray at the temple of Golu devta in Almora. He is worshipped as a king who dispenses justice, and people come and hang their affidavits and court proceedings in the temple. My prayers are answered.

The hearing goes on and on, but in the week of Prime Minister Narendra Modi's swearing in, the order finally comes, quashing charges against me and the others. I am told that in its note to the law ministry on 5 August 2015, the CBI said that after due examination of the order of the Delhi High Court, it had decided that this was not a fit matter for filing an appeal by way of special leave petition in the Supreme Court of India.

Thus ends the Official Secrets Act case against us. It wasn't so much the charges that were scary, but the whole grind of it—the fees to the lawyers, the wasted time, the mental attrition, and the unnecessary creation of judicial caseload.

We were the pilot project of the right-wing vendetta machine.

## VIP STYLE

Within ten days of going public with Operation West End, the Delhi Police sends a security contingent for Tarun and me.

Apparently, there are some gangsters armed with AK-47s who are out to polish us off. Basically—the story goes—an ISI cell, in concert with an Indian MP, has devised a plan to kill us so that the blame falls on the Atal Behari Vajpayee government, which is on a tremendously sticky wicket because of our story. The Congress has stalled Parliament for more than three weeks over the issue—the most for any single topic after 1947.

For a party that claims to be the face of corruption-free politics, the story is the first big jolt. The BJP is no longer Teflon-coated. After our story, other scams appear in quick succession: the UTI scam, the stock-market scam, and on and on.

For the first time in history, Indian citizens get to see visuals of 'corruption in practice' on their television sets. Before this, corruption featured as drawing-room talk, but now, a media website has shown the ruling party president nonchalantly grabbing one lakh rupees on camera, like it is the most natural thing to do. Not to mention talking about wanting to be paid off in dollars.

At first, I write a letter to the Ministry of Home Affairs refusing security and pointing out that if there is indeed a threat, our reporter Mathew Samuel deserves to be protected too. A week later, at Tarun's insistence, I relent, and soon have an escort car with two gunmen following mine. A third man sits with me, with a handgun. The rest have sub-machine guns. As a result of my intervention, Samuel gets security as well.

Having security changes your life. For one, there are fewer seats available in your car. They get to see everybody you meet. You have to factor their shift changes into your schedule. And get used to the stares you attract when you have gunmen hanging around you.

You also have to start taking care of those who guard you at night. Quite frequently, your neighbours complain about your security cover's noisy habits. The night guards sit about gossiping till late in the night.

You have to be careful about what all this does to your head. I can feel my sense of self-importance shooting up within a week. One day, I quietly visit the Lodi crematorium and watch a line of dead bodies burning. It's a reminder of the common end waiting for all of us, and from that day on, I am totally indifferent to my guards, except for attending to their legitimate needs.

I discover that the guards assigned for my protection are an excellent source of gossip about politicians, as they have been part of security details attached to many of them. The politicians, however, have very different ideas about what their security cover is for. Early on, I am embarrassed by one of my guards 'shooing' away people in front of me while I walk to the Bahrisons bookstore in Delhi's Khan Market. I am so aghast that I immediately have a chat with the guard and his supervisor. They apologise. The guard says that in his previous details with politicians, this is what was expected.

As a journalist under protection, I can't meet my sources openly any longer, for fear of their privacy being compromised. These are the days before encrypted voice calls.

The security lasts for about eight years, on and off, and I develop some great friendships with some of my guards.

Once, while I'm under Delhi Police protection, the officer investigating the case against us under the Official Secrets Act comes to our office, and an argument ensues because he is not carrying a valid notice. Our lawyers have advised us to engage with the authorities whenever called, but never informally. The officer goes and complains at the Malviya Nagar Police Station, and lo and behold, the Delhi Police have a handle to arrest me on an obstruction charge.

The constables guarding me notice a few members of the other team surreptitiously checking out my residence. They confront them and discover that they are Delhi Police colleagues. My guards warn the interlopers off saying, in effect, that if they act dodgy around here again, they will open fire, warrant or no warrant. This scares the Malviya Nagar cops so much that they shelve their plan of arresting me at home ... and pick me up from my office instead.

Much later, even during times when there's no immediate danger, my former guards occasionally drop by my office or home to ask if I feel threatened in any way. They say they are willing to come by and do some unofficial guard duty. I decline politely without offending them.

## A LIVE-STREAMED ARREST

In 2002, police from the Malviya Nagar thana arrest me from the *Tehelka* office in Soami Nagar. A CBI officer has charged me with obstruction of justice. When the police pick me up, I ring up Uday Shankar, the editor at AajTak, and he immediately takes the call and airs my voice live on his channel.

As the police take me away in their jeep, I answer questions from the news anchor on my mobile. In effect, you have the spectacle of my arrest being live-streamed on a major news channel. Actually, I must compliment the Delhi Police for not impounding my phone and stopping the live broadcast.

The police keep telling me that they have nothing to do with the situation and are helpless in the case of a political arrest. They take me for a medical test at the All India Institute of Medical Sciences (AIIMS), then produce me before a judge, Reema Singh Nag, at Patiala House. She grants me bail, but on the condition that I surrender my passport to the court.

As I leave the first-floor courtroom, I flash a V-sign from a balcony for the television cameras waiting for me downstairs. Later, I give them a rather screechy sound bite. Uday reprimands me later, saying a flustered bite never works well on television.

I am back at the *Tehelka* office by late afternoon. It feels surreal.

The action-packed day turned out well only because a judge stood up to the ruling government and granted bail immediately.

In those days, the media had the gumption to call a story the way it was. And the judiciary provided protection to whistleblowers against state excesses. Both are rare now.

## A FAMILIAR FACE

After Krishna Prasad and I break the cricket match-fixing story in 1997, which I subsequently follow up with several other match-fixing exposés, my face becomes rather well known because of the many print and TV interviews. After the May 2000 exposé, where we help former all-rounder Manoj Prabhakar do his own exposing, it becomes even more recognisable.

Operation West End takes this to a different level. Random people accost me and start chatting. Many don't remember my name but recall that I am associated with *Tehelka*.

Once, I am with my wife and kids in Sentosa Island, Singapore, waiting for a show to start, when it starts raining cats and dogs. My family makes off with our two umbrellas, and I scamper over to a cold-drink vendor's stall, where another man is sheltering under a sheet of plastic. It doesn't offer much protection—there is just enough space for me to squeeze in.

The other man turns around and regards me coolly. 'Good evening, Aniruddha,' he says. I am too thrown to do anything but grin. I learn he is from Calcutta and studying in Singapore.

Once, when I'm in Prague, in the midst of a tiff with the chap at a money-exchange shop, an Indian man troops by and on seeing me, stops to ask, 'Do you need any help, Aniruddha?'

He can't do anything, really. The money changers in Prague take crookery to another level.

Another time, I'm filling up a fast-track visa form in Bangkok, well past midnight. I have a fever, I'm shivering, and a hoodie conceals half my face. Somebody taps me on the shoulder—'Aren't you from *Tehelka*?' It's well past my *Tehelka* days, but I have to nod my head.

A few times, I even get upgraded to business class on flights because the airline duty manager recognises me and is a fan of my work. These are among the more welcome consequences of being recognised.

## MEASURING CORRUPTION

One of the best compliments I've ever received is for my work on Operation West End.

Sometime in March or April of 2001, I receive a call from one of my friends in Bangalore. She tells me that she was out on a walk, a few days after our exposé, when she overheard a few labourers talking to each other on the street. One woman was explaining to the others what *Tehelka* was. She said that *Tehelka* was a big electronic machine that had been built in Delhi—if you stood in front of it, the machine would immediately tell you the amount of corruption you had indulged in, in the course of your life!

I laugh for days afterwards, and the anecdote brings a smile to my face even now. For the story to have penetrated to that level is quite a feat.

A *Tehelka* staffer narrates another incident. He was taking the bus to office and happened to be present during a huge altercation between a passenger and the conductor. The passenger felt that the conductor was overcharging him. As he got off the bus, he continued to argue, shouting loudly that that he would report the incident to *Tehelka*!

When people ask me whether the *Tehelka* story was worth the trouble, I cite these two tales as compensation enough.

## MY BOSSES

My first boss in my career as a journalist was Tarun Tejpal. When he recruited me, he was an associate editor at the *India Today* magazine, handling the book review and essay pages as well as some back-of-the-book features.

Tarun, apart from being an excellent writer and editor, also had the knack of getting some of the best writers for *India Today* and, subsequently, *Outlook* magazine, where he was part of the launch team. He never micromanaged a story, preferring to give you guidance in broad strokes. His USP as a journalist, apart from being a good one himself, was to manage interpersonal relationships, leaving reporters to chase their own stuff.

*India Today* soon had a new copy editor, Amrit Dhillon, who came from the BBC and was another excellent boss to have. She had a great sense of copy and carried forward the rewrite tradition introduced in Indian journalism by the likes of Dilip Bobb and Inderjit Badhwar.

When I moved to *Down to Earth*, my boss was Uday Shankar. Shankar had come to the magazine from the *Times of India*, having contributed a great deal to the State of India's Environment reports that the Centre for Science and Environment brought out under the legendary Anil Agarwal.

Shankar was another boss who left you alone to do whatever you were up to. He could hold forth on theories about the government's economic policy as it related to the country's environment policy, throwing up insights that made you look at things afresh. When Shankar left print and went to television, he decided early on never to become an anchor—a decision that contributed to his success at both India Today and Star News.

In India, many television channels suffer from naming their star anchor as the editorial head. The anchor's energies are largely directed towards cementing their own careers and shows, rather than the editorial well-being of the entire platform. AajTak understood this pitfall early on, and seldom had their editor-in-chief anchor a show on air.

One thing about my bosses. They have all had a wicked sense of humour. Tarun even more than the others.

## BUNKER 13

In October 1996, I take two months off from *Outlook* magazine to begin a new novel. It is a thriller set in Kashmir and Delhi, written in the second person.

I write up 90 per cent of the novel but can't finish it in time. When I ask for a third month of unpaid leave, Mehta asks me, drily, whether I want to retain my job.

So I rejoin. And Rhea, my eldest child, comes along three weeks later. With that ends all peace and quiet.

I send Gillon the first three chapters of *Bunker 13*, and he immediately signs me on as an author he will represent himself.

On each trip to India, Gillon urges me to finish the novel. But journalism keeps me busy; Mehta has given me a lot of leeway at the magazine, and I am travelling all over the place.

In 2002, we throw a celebratory dinner for Sir V.S. Naipaul in New Delhi, when he wins the Nobel Prize in literature. Gillon tears into me once again, and says I am wasting my time and talent doing stupid stuff like *Tehelka* and that I have to get down to writing. He says I am a born writer and anything else I do is just an add-on.

In a burst of energy over a few weeks, and in between our legal battles, I finish *Bunker 13*. Within a week, Gillon gets an offer of £80,000 pounds from Faber & Faber for the British and Commonwealth rights and, soon after that, $250,000 from Farrar, Straus and Giroux for the North American rights. The agency goes on to sell several other language rights.

In December 2003, London's *Literary Review* announces that I have been awarded its Bad Sex in Fiction Award for certain passages in *Bunker 13*. The award has been bestowed in the past on Salman Rushdie, John Updike and Christopher Bollen, among others. Rarely have authors gone to collect it in person, for there is a reading session at the event, where he is roasted. But I agree to go as Sting is presenting the award, and it is a free ticket to London along with a hotel at Tottenham Court Road. I also prepare my own shaky response, to be read amidst the babble.

Gillon Aitken has prepped me, advising me against taking direct pot shots at the *Literary Review*. He tells me they always have about fifty stooges planted in the audience, who will begin booing the moment I start making things a little hairy for them.

Some years later, I bump into Sting and his partner at Indira Gandhi International airport in Delhi. He is on his way to Jaipur. We laugh together about the 2003 awards.

# PASSPORT BLUES

In 2003, after my novel is published in the UK and the US, the publishers want me to travel to New York, Los Angeles and London to promote the book. Later, I am to go to Barcelona for the launch of the Spanish edition.

Each time, I have to submit my travel itinerary to the court and petition it to release my passport for the trip. I am granted permission but, very often, have to face verbal opposition from the prosecutor.

The court clerks mob me for baksheesh every time I get an order in my favour, as they are the ones who physically hand over my passport to me. It's a strange feature of the Indian mentality, this baksheesh. I have even seen peons in North and South Block accost people for money after they emerge from their appointments with bureaucrats and ministers.

After several such petitions, I move the Delhi High Court to amend the bail condition of the lower court, and my appeal is upheld. But I often wonder how the courts would react these days to requests for granting such basic freedoms as travel, when there are so many people fleeing the country after defrauding banks of thousands of crores.

# PART III

'All journalism should be investigative, from football to cookery.'

—John Pilger

# THE BIRTH OF COBRAPOST

I leave *Tehelka* in the middle of 2003. I had made a commitment to myself to steer the organisation out of the Justice Venkataswami Commission of Inquiry, and am relieved to have seen everyone's testimony through. But ever since we broke the story, the NDA government has engaged us in one witch-hunt after another, and after heading the legal response to all of this, I am drained. I have also done very little journalism since the story broke.

It's also clear that Tarun wants to take *Tehelka* in a different direction. I want to stick to hard-core investigation and somehow create a model that will help sustain that. Tarun's vision is more rounded: he wants all the trappings of a big media platform.

The distance between us is also growing. Tarun's becoming more of an 'I' person. I am more a 'we' person. At some point, I began to feel, rightly or wrongly, that he is taking more credit for Operation West End than is deserved. Of course, I will outgrow all of that over the years—the lust of the byline, so to speak. But for now, this rankles, as do many other little things, which are best left alone.

In the end, I give up all my equity in the company to Tarun, with the understanding that he might give me a return in five years if the company does well and that *Tehelka* will take care of all pending legal expenses. Of course, I never get anything out of my investment. I hold around 16 per cent of the company, or a bit less, when I leave. Tarun eventually shuts the company and transfers the brand name to a new company—a decision I am fairly upset about at the time.

Professional ethics notwithstanding, Tarun is the best editor I have worked with. His understanding of a media product is superb, and his writing incredible. He is also one of the few people I really enjoy sharing a laugh with, simply because of our keen sense of the absurd in daily life. We also have a lot of common memories from over the years.

After leaving *Tehelka*, I find it imperative to start a website where I can pursue investigative journalism. With the government coming at us hammer and tongs, I feel I need a news platform to get stories out, in spite of the trouble I might get into. That's how I establish Cobrapost in 2003. Initially, it is just a news links platform with very few original stories. But gradually, we begin to do investigations and sign content contracts with news channels. I choose the name 'Cobrapost' because it has high recall value. In Indian mythology, serpents are guardians of both wealth and knowledge.

## ASHA PAREKH IN IRAQ

In 2004, I enter Iraq through Kuwait. I want to travel through several countries in the Middle East and write a travelogue. The book never happens, but I end up doing some interesting pieces for *Outlook* while I am travelling in the region. I embed with American troops in a camp in Baghdad, get thrown out of their mess for wearing sandals, experience first-hand the panic of a false mortar attack, and travel to Kurdish areas, Jordan, Israel and the West Bank, where I try and fail to meet Yasser Arafat.

Driving down from Kuwait to Basra is an adventure. Having made an arrangement with a Shia sheikh to drive me up to Basra and then onwards to Baghdad, I spend the first night at his house in Basra. It isn't advisable to stay in hotels, as the kidnapping of foreigners is very frequent. Truck drivers ferrying supplies for the American troops have become targets for Iraqi insurgents. Since April 2004, organised Iraqi gangs and militia have begun to attack convoys on a regular basis. A lot of these convoys have Indian drivers, and my arrival in Iraq coincides with the kidnapping of some Indian truck drivers by Iraqi militia. It appears that a few Indian companies have won labour contracts in Iraqi cities from American entities, and have employed Indians from the Gulf to service these contracts, thus making them vulnerable to the Iraqi militia, who view them as enablers of the American occupation of Iraq.

There are scores of Indians in this part of the world, risking their lives for salaries ranging from $300 to $1500 a month. Working as cooks, kitchen helpers, guards and truck drivers, these men are willing to put their lives on the line. The money is possibly much more than what they would earn back home. The sheer desperation of it is tragic.

At the Indian embassy in Baghdad, I encounter about fourteen Indians from Punjab who have paid agents for a passage to Europe, but have instead found themselves dumped in Iraq at the height of the insurgency. A handful of them have repeated the mistake about three times. The Indian embassy is on a collection drive to pay for their airfare back home.

Meanwhile, four kidnapped Indian truck drivers need to be rescued, and I hear that the Indian embassy is in touch with a certain Sheikh Hisham al Dulaimi to broker a release with the militants.

Dulaimi, it turns out, is pretty shady and hard to track down. He's one of those guys who exist in the shadows. And yet, a love of the limelight can suddenly draw them out into the open. After a lot of trouble, I end up locating him at an ongoing tribal council meeting in Baghdad and interview him. A bulky man, he reeks of cigars and caffeine.

Dulaimi assesses me. '*Hind Sahafi?*' he asks. Are you a journalist from India?

'Yes,' I say.

He says he is in touch with the kidnappers, and there has been an exchange of notes. He says he is appreciative of India and fond of its culture, so he is doing his best. He is a lover of fine things, he says. And he is also fond of Indian cine stars. Especially Asha Parekh.

'What would it take to release the prisoners faster? What would hasten the process?' I ask.

Dulaimi slaps his thigh and names Asha Parekh.

'What would your reaction be if she were to call you herself and request your full cooperation for the release of the hostages?' I dig further.

'The hostages would be released today. If she calls me herself, that's what will happen,' Dulaimi boasts.

He has previously denied knowing the identity of the kidnappers, so he quickly qualifies: 'I mean, her saying something will have an effect on the kidnappers also. Not me alone. Also, if other Indian actors like Amitabh Bachchan and Dharmendra go on television and request not only me but other Iraqis to solve the problem, then the drivers should be released.'

The *Outlook* report is picked up by wire agencies in India, and reporters rush to the cine stars, asking whether they would be willing to call Dulaimi. The Indian embassy soon drops him as a go-between, saying he is not 'serious'.

# THE KURDISH DISCO DANCER

In 2004, at the height of the insurgency in Iraq, I see four hoardings of Shahrukh Khan in Baghdad, advertising soft drinks. I don't know if they are authorised or not, but talking to families there gives me a sense of the immense penetration of Indian cinema and stars in Iraq.

I even spot the hoardings in Erbil, the capital of the Kurdish region. There are shops there that sell pirated CDs of Hindi films.

I land up at one such shop, to do a general enquiry about how many DVDs or CDs are sold, how the business works, stuff like that. The shopkeeper takes to me enthusiastically once he gathers that I am an Indian. He warms to the topic of Bollywood.

On this visit, I have a Kurdish bodyguard with me 24/7. Appointed to keep me safe during my three-day trip by the police themselves, he is armed with an AK-47.

The bodyguard is also strangely animated while I ask the shopkeeper questions about Hindi films and TV serials. He wants to contribute too. So I ask him, through my interpreter, whether he, too, likes Bollywood films.

'Yes, of course, sir, I do,' he answers bashfully in Kurdish, much to my amusement. My Kurdish translator is all smiles.

I ask him what his favourite Indian movie is. And I will never forget the scene when, for the first time in days, he sets his AK-47 down and suddenly breaks into a dance.

I gape at his vigorous moves, hardly able to keep a straight face. His enthusiasm is infectious.

'This is from *Disco Dancer*, by Mithun,' he says, beaming at me.

He remembers the name of the film and the actor! I find it hilarious that a big, burly Kurdish fighter has as one of his idols the svelte and urbane Mithun, with his flamboyant groove and white, flashy jacket.

That is the soft power of Bollywood for you.

## WHAT DID VAJPAYEE THINK?

Sometime in 2005, I have a long conversation with Namita, the adopted daughter of former prime minister Atal Behari Vajpayee, at solicitor Ryan Karanjiwala's dinner party. At one point, I ask her what Vajpayee-ji thought of the *Tehelka* exposé. She replies: 'It never came up as a topic, but one day the TV was on, and he was watching it. You were on air addressing some press conference or the other, and he turned around and said to me, "Aisey log bahut kum rah gaye hain."' There are very few people like him now.

## THE MATCH-FIXING CONFESSIONAL

In 2005, I do another cricket match-fixing scoop for *Outlook* magazine. To give a bit of context: in July 2000, income tax officers had conducted countrywide raids under Operation Gentleman. They went after the who's who of the Indian cricketing establishment, and the entire affair was linked to the match-fixing inquiry being conducted by the CBI. One of the documents seized from a home in Bombay was a facsimile sent by former India captain Mohammed Azharuddin. The intended recipient appeared to be Sangeeta Bijlani. Consisting of many pages in Azharuddin's own handwriting, it was his recollection of what transpired when the CBI's match-fixing investigation team grilled him for nearly eight hours. It seemed Azharuddin was recollecting events so that his lawyer could assess the situation.

In the document, Azharuddin admitted to his links with mafia don Abu Salem, a host of Indian cricketers, including Ajay Sharma, Ajay Jadeja and Nayan Mongia, and bookies like the famous Mukesh K. Gupta, whom he introduced to the former South African captain Hansie Cronje. He also took potshots at Sunny Gavaskar and a certain Sachin. The Gavaskar potshot was related to Gavaskar telling Manoj Prabhakar during the *Tehelka* investigation into match-fixing that Azharuddin had fallen short of money for a watch in Zimbabwe and had somebody transfer US $10,000 to him.

After the inquiry, the BCCI ended up issuing a life ban on some players, including Azharuddin. The CBI made their preliminary inquiry public in 2000, but it never gave away the details. You could say that my 2005 story was the first ever confessional by a cricketer regarding his involvement in match-fixing, after Hansie Cronje.

I am reproducing here the interview as it was published in *Outlook* magazine. The excerpts are exact reproductions from Azhar's handwritten note—with errors and oddities of language intact. It is in a question-answer format devised by him to explain what transpired between him and the CBI. When contacted, all Azhar could came up with was 'I can't remember these things.'

### Azhar on Ratan Mehta

He is a very big bookie and he is also involved in the narcotics and drugs. He is very close to Ajay Jadeja (of which they have tapes of him in conversation with Ajay Jadeja). He is also close to the Pakistan team. In fact, the whole Pakistan team went to RM restaurant in Delhi. RM's sister Mona Mehta is also involved.

**Q: The CBI asked me about RM?**
A: I told them I don't know anybody by this name as I genuinely never heard about him or know him. The CBI was very keen that I tell them I know him, but the other officer interfered and said that he had spoken to RM sister and she said that they don't know Azharuddin.

### Azhar on Shoban Mehta

The CBI asked me do you know him, I said no. I really don't know him. Suddenly one officer said, who's the cricketer who got a very expensive necklace for his wife, I said that is for you to find out, I am only narrating what I read in the newspaper. (One of my friends in Hyd has confirmed that Shoban Mehta has links with Sachin and deals with him regularly).

### Azhar on Ajay Sharma

**Q: How you know him**
A: I told them he was the captain of Delhi Cricket team for a long time, my roommate when playing for India.

**Q: Why was Ajay Sharma calling you 8 to 10 times only before the matches not otherwise?**
A: I told them that his son was not well and he was trying to get in touch. The CBI told me that though he was calling you, but after he called you, Ajay was calling a lots of bookies in Delhi. I told CBI that I was not aware what he does in his

private life and it doesn't concern me. They refused to believe me. (The only problem I have is with this Ajay Sharma.) (I told the CBI that I took money 10 lakhs for providing information in three games. I also told the CBI that I talked to Mongia and Ajay Jadeja about this. 1. Sri Lanka vs India in 1997. 2. India vs South Africa in Rajkot 1996 Titan Cup. 3. India vs Pakistan in Jaipur in 1999). The CBI told me that Ajay Sharma's wife called your residence in Bombay quite a few times but you didn't talk to her. The CBI says that Ajay Sharma is your good friend but how come he is not calling you 8 to 10 times nowadays. If Ajay is your good friend, he should call you because you are under a lot of strain and stress.

### Azhar on Sunil Gavaskar

Q: Whether you had called for money from Sanjeev Kalra 10,000 dollars.
A: I had not called for money from any person. It was Sunil Gavaskar who wanted to get money from his friend some Kalra, because he had said that on many occasions he has got money from Kalra and one phone call from him & 10,000$ will come instantly. I refuse to take Sunil Gavaskar's offer. I don't know whether SG got the money & I do not know what he did with it because I never bought a watch.

### Azhar on Ravi Shastri

It is all fake and fabricated and he has a personal grudge against me for last so many years. He is been trying to pull me down and malign me. This is also clear from his talk to Prabhakar on Tehelka.com where he says Azhar ko to fix karna chhahiye. This buying of watch is all crap, nonsense and rubbish. Mr Butani has already clarified and I am informed that he is going to take him to court for false statement.

**Azhar on Mukesh Gupta**

I know him, I introduced him to Cronje as a jeweller after that what they spoke I really don't know at all. I didn't tell Cronje that he was a bookie.

**Q: The CBI asked me whether you know MK?**
**A:** I said who is this MK, they said we know it is 4 years back, but take your time, think and answer, but I still maintained that I didn't know him. They got me to see the photograph of him, but still I said no, then they put pressure on me verbally and even got me to see the records of MK's stay in the Land Mark hotel in Kanpur with all the stay records, where and which room he was staying and they said even now if you say no we have witnesses from the Land Mark hotel who has seen you and Cronje with MK. The CBI told me that you are lucky you are not directly involved but there are others who are directly involved. The CBI said that MK is in their custody and will call him so that you can see for yourself. The CBI even told me that MK is not in touch with me for the last 2½ years. The CBI asked me who introduce MK to you I said Ajay Sharma. Their information is up to the mark. The CBI said we are not going by Tehelka.com or by any other reports we go by what we have. I had no choice but to tell the truth.

## Azhar on Abu Salem

**Q: They asked me whether you know him.**
A: I said no, then they said that during the Chandigarh match in 1996 you spoke to him, I said I don't know and have not spoken to him. They said he offered you 1.25 cr to fix a match. I said no. I kept lying to them all the time. In the end they played the tapes of him talking to me. It was very embarrassing. I told them that when these people call you have to talk to them otherwise the consequences are bad and life threatening. Luckily for me I was the man of the match in that match and India won the game. The CBI said that we do understand that these things happen. I refused to agree to Abu Salem's offer. The CBI was aware of that as they had heard that on the tape. The CBI also said that they have hundreds of tapes of film stars, directors and producers who talk to them very regularly. The CBI told me not to speak to these people any more. I clearly told them that was the only time I spoke to these people.

## Azhar on #ay Gupta, #meesh Gupta, Gyan Chand Gupta

**Q: They asked how you know these people.**
A: I said I met them in a hotel in Delhi, they said how you can get friendly with them just like that and not others who meet you everyday. I told them they were very nice people. The CBI said you met them through Ajay Sharma. That is the truth and I had no choice but to confirm. The CBI has even got details of his shopping list in Harrods in England, they even saw me in Harrods with him shopping. The CBI says that you and him are photographed in the camera of

Harrods. I told CBI that, I know him and went with him for shopping. The CBI says that Ajay Gupta spent 50 lakhs in the shopping. I don't know how they have this information. I presume they must have interrogated him. The CBI says that they have spoken to him as well. The CBI also knows that I had gone to his house once for dinner. They also confirmed that he is not a bookie just a businessman who likes betting. The CBI also knows that I once gave Ajay Gupta to get a pending license for a petrol station, since they are in the petrol station business.

The CBI asked me about Sunil Devnani. I said he is my classmate from Hyd and he is heading the Sivaki Electronics in Dubai. The CBI says that why his tel no is not registered under his personal name. Even I didn't know this. The CBI told me it is registered under some Arab's name. I explained to the CBI that when you do business in Dubai you have to have a local sponsor, so he must be his local sponsor. That was all.

The CBI asked me about Asif Iqbal. I said I know him because of cricket. Does he speak to you. I said on and off not regularly.

They asked me about Ravi Shastri and Butani episode on Tehelka.com. I told them that it was false and I had a letter to clarify. The CBI asked me why cricketers are against you. I told them they have personal grudges and jealous and he also thinks that I was the person who was responsible for removing them from the team.

In the end when I asked them if I could travel abroad they told me enjoy yourself and be normal and said if you have any problems please don't hesitate to call us.

### Azhar on Manoj-Kapil Affair

He never ever disclosed to me or even came to me or talk to me in this matter.

**Q: Why everybody is targeting me?**
A: Mainly because I am from minority community. I am being victimised and targeted...specially some ex-cricketers raising fingers against me to settle their personal grudges and they can't stand the idea that a person from the minority community should be in the saddle of Indian Cricket specially when I have remained there for 16 years. I appeal to all the public not to be swayed away by the misinformation about me spread by the media, vilification campaign carried out against me in order to dislodge me and to create dispathy (sic) in the minds of the public. I am not the man who declared 16 crore in the vdis Scheme.

(Courtesy: *Outlook*)

## CASH FOR QUESTIONS

'Has the Government given sanction for the seed trial of Salinger Cotton of Monsanto? If so, has the report been prepared on Catch-22 cotton so far?'

Dateline: 12 December 2005

In March 2005, I write a column for the *Hindustan Times* on a series that a news channel has run on the casting couch. It seems to me an exercise in voyeurism—hardly something that justifies the use of a hidden camera. I suggest some stories I feel actually warrant the use of hidden cameras. One is an investigation of how some MPs take money to ask questions in Parliament. In many ways, MPs asking questions in Parliament is the original exercise of the Right to Information (RTI). The various ministries have to answer, and it was once the only way to get information out of an opaque system.

After the column is published, I receive a notice from Parliament, asking me to explain myself as I have denigrated the institution, according to them. The *Hindustan Times* quickly apologises and washes its hands off the column, dumping all the grief on me. This only provokes me to actually investigate the story. There are many middlemen in Lutyens' Delhi, and they know exactly which MPs are in the 'business'. These middlemen ultimately open the door for reporter Suhasini Raj.

We float a fictitious organisation called the North India Small Manufacturers' Association (NISMA). Suhasini, posing as a functionary of NISMA, lobbies to table certain questions in Parliament that will benefit her association in some way.

Without blinking, the MPs we approach bring scores of questions on our behalf before the House, some starred, some not. They even get answers for us. Some MPs are only too happy to put themselves at NISMA's service. A BJP MP, for example, offers to table as many questions as NISMA has for him. His price: fifty grand a month. Ironically, some of the parliamentarians who readily pocket the money are publicly piqued about how corrupt politicians are.

Over three sessions of Parliament, various MPs table questions. When we break the story, in partnership with AajTak, on 12 December 2005, about sixty questions have been submitted by eleven MPs, out of which about twenty-five questions have been actually tabled.

Some of the questions we frame are absolutely bizarre, designed to bring out the ludicrous nature of the whole process. We ask the railway ministry:

- Has it placed any order for the Yossarian Electro Diesel Engine from Germany?
- Is the Ministry aware that the Tom Wolfe Committee Report in Germany has halted its induction into the Euro rail system?

Yossarian, of course, is the principal character in Joseph Heller's classic novel, *Catch-22*, and Tom Wolfe is the author of *The Bonfire of the Vanities*.

For the Ministry of Civil Aviation, we have a different set of questions:

- Is the government aware that a domestic flying license had been denied to Cobra Cargo for starting its India operations?
- When did Semper Sursum Private Limited, the holding company of Cobra Cargo, apply for the domestic cargo license?

*Semper Sursum* (Latin for 'aim high') is the motto of my school, St Joseph's College, in Allahabad. Initially, I considered calling the story Operation Semper Sursum. But Aroon Purie, editor-in-chief of TV Today Network, found it archaic, so we decided to call the investigation Operation Duryodhana, as the name would catch on among both English and Hindi speakers. One newspaper actually publishes this anecdote about the investigation's name, prompting calls from the alumni of my school—and many a private laugh over it.

Here are some other absurd questions we get away with in Parliament:

- Has the ministry lifted the 1962 ban it imposed on the book *For Whom the Bell Tolls* by Ernest Hemingway and the 1975

ban on Ken Kesey's book *One Flew Over the Cuckoo's Nest* and Hunter Thompson's book *Fear and Loathing in Las Vegas*?
+ If so, when were the bans removed?
+ Is it true that while NRI firms such as India Uncut of USA, Sepia Mutiny of Britain and AnarCap Lib of the Netherlands have been allowed to invest in Indian small-scale industries, the reputed German investment firm Desipundit has been denied permission? If so, what are the reasons thereof? Is the Government of India planning to automate the long permission procedure for small-scale industries to import new technologies such as trackbacks, pingbacks, blogrolls, splogs and hit counters?
+ Has the government given sanction for the seed trial of Salinger Cotton of Monsanto? If so, has the report been prepared on Catch-22 cotton so far?

I think we even get an answer for that last question, with only a slight modification by the question-setting department.

I still wonder how these questions passed muster in the screening process and made their way to the House. A little bit of common sense would have done us in, but that is a very rare commodity among politicians. Perhaps their greed inures them to it, and so they failed to realise that we were pulling a fast one on them.

There are some close moments for us, though. A BJP MP becomes suspicious when we can't recall the name of the MP from Moradabad, where NISMA is supposedly based. He wants to check Suhasini's bag and we have to make a hasty exit. The same MP later lands up at my house to 'negotiate' a deal so he can go scot free.

One MP throws an indecent proposal at Suhasini. Offering to bring other MPs on board for free, he says with the nonchalance of a seasoned lecher: '*Aapke paas deh hai na?*' You have your body to offer, don't you?

Both the Lok Sabha and the Rajya Sabha launch enquiries into Operation Duryodhana. The Lok Sabha MPs are advised by Speaker Somnath Chatterjee not to attend Parliament till such time as the Pawan Kumar Bansal Committee submits its report. Chatterjee also invites me for a chat to his residence. I know him from my *Tehelka* days, when he had once offered to do the closing arguments for us at the *Tehelka* inquiry commission.

Chatterjee stays in the Speaker's house, near the Park Hotel roundabout that leads to Jantar Mantar. At his residence, he sheds his formal demeanour with me. He presents me with a Parker pen and says, 'Well done.' He asks some questions about our investigation. He is particularly keen to know whether more MPs are involved, apart from the eleven we have already exposed. There are no others, I tell him.

Suhasini and I are soon deposing to the Bansal Committee and the Rajya Sabha-appointed committee. The chairman of the Rajya Sabha committee is Dr Karan Singh, and its members include Sushma Swaraj, Bimal Jalan and Jay Panda. Jalan wants to know the procedure we followed while approaching certain MPs. He is under the impression that we cold called the MPs, as if we used a telephone directory. He finds it hard to understand that it is the middlemen in North and South Block who took us to meet the MPs who they 'knew' were in play for this sort of thing.

Soon afterwards, all eleven MPs are dismissed.

On occasion, our system does produce a commendable degree of accountability. But the instances are few and far between. In fact, Cobrapost does two more stories concerning MPs—one in 2010 and another in 2013—that show our lawmakers' propensity for corruption.

# SUICIDE BOMBERS

I'm still tickled by the sheer audacity of some of the stories we do in association with Star News. One is on the notorious D-Company, and it shows Fahim Machmach, one of Dawood's henchmen, targeting small-time businessmen in Mumbai. The tape we receive from our sources gives a chilling account of how the gang keeps tabs on the activities of its victims and their relations before swooping down on them for ransom. Somewhat ironically, the victims of such extortions are Muslims.

Another story we cover in 2006 involves footage we receive of suicide bombers preparing for an imminent attack in November 2004. Their target was Prime Minister Manmohan Singh, who was then visiting Kashmir. The video shows a young lad barely out of his teens, Abu Umair, and his accomplice, making preparations in their hideout in the Bandipora jungles. One of them is dressed as a Sikh. The camera captures Chhota Bilal, a terrorist involved in many attacks, entering the room and conversing with the boys. Finally, Salahuddin, the young commander of the Laskhar-e-Taiba, enters, armed with a Kalashnikov. We also see Shamsheer and Harris, two other terrorists. When the boys leave the hideout, they are ready with fake identity cards and a camera, masquerading as employees of a local news channel. They ask questions of people they meet on their way to the venue. The video was shot by Shabbir Bukhari, a lawyer, and his friend Shaqeel Sofi, who were the boys' local handlers. As it happened, both terrorists were killed in an encounter at the Suleman Complex, close to the stadium, before D-day.

## THE ORIGINAL DATA STORY

We often hear talk these days about how our personal data is being traded for money by corporate entities that are supposed to protect it. Many years before Cambridge Analytica and the breaching of Aadhaar data became a common occurrence, we released, on Star News, the story of an undercover investigation that the *Sun* had broken in the UK. The story showed Karan Bahari and Sushant Chandok from the Indian BPO industry trading customers' personal details, bank accounts and credit card details, along with passwords and codes, for money. It was a story ahead of its time.

### 'HELLO, WELCOME, ME THE TONY B!'

Sometime in 2007, I start developing a film script, the tentative title of which is 'Ali: The Pakistani Spy Comes to Make Propaganda film about Country India and Make Problem'. It is based on real interviews, Ali G style, and I want to be Ali, the protagonist, as I feel I have a degree in absurd humour!

I pitch the idea to several people, and though they like it, nobody wants to put in the money.

Meanwhile, to develop my skills, I do *The Tony B Show* for Channel V. Along the lines of Ali G, I interview politicians, fashion designers, singers, cricketers and other celebrities with a made-up persona. I wear a wig and big glasses and ask baseless questions in an equally made-up accent, which they take seriously. They all are under the impression that it is a formal interview, and so when I start asking absurd questions with a straight face, they are left guessing whether I'm a duffer or pulling a fast one on them.

Apart from questions related to their line of work, I toss in queries about current affairs, the environment, the holy cow, and other such things. Many of my interviewees are ill-informed, yet so pompous that they proffer answers to sound brainy. It is fun to watch them reel under the onslaught of absurdities, squirming and smirking at the same time.

Those encounters still make me chuckle.

Although it all depends on who I'm interviewing on a given day, some of my standard questions are:

- There was a United Nations conference on global warming in Bali in 2007. India's huge cattle population is causing this warming. So India has committed to reducing its herds by half by 2010. What do you say?
- About three hundred human skeletons have been discovered in Nandigram. Dalai Lama says an all-faith monument should be built at the site. What do you think?
- The government has offered China a naval base on Indian soil. Do you think the Chinese should reciprocate by giving India an air base in Xinjiang?

My guests' gumption makes for some amusing moments. For instance, singer Shibani Kashyap has no clue about Nandigram and the Dalai Lama's supposed statement. When I ask for her opinion, she says, 'Oh yes, we must do what such a noble soul calls for. But he needs the support of the whole world.' On allowing China a naval base on Indian soil, Kashyap speaks like a foreign policy expert: 'Yes, but … I think, any sort of help from us … it could be economical, it could (sic) socio-economy.' She even has lofty ideas about how India could cull its cattle population:

turn jungles into sanctuaries. But when it comes to talking music, Kashyap becomes a cat on a hot tin roof. 'I should not look like a fool ... I will not be able to take this interview further,' she declares fretfully, turning to me and the crew. I try to persuade her to continue, only to get a lesson in etiquette: '*Vinamrata se baat kijiye.*' Talk to me politely!

It is fun interviewing Kailash Kher who, like Kashyap, loses his patience. But, unlike her, the Sufi singer does not lose his civility and polite demeanour. In fact, I give Kher enough reasons to act the way he does. A few minutes into the interview, he is at a complete loss when I tell him, nonsensically, that Dhrupad is Pandit Bhimsen Joshi's favourite raga. Quoting from a fictitious autobiography of Ravi Shankar, I ask if Kher agrees that 'Sometimes you feel *sa re ga ma* is not enough basis ... that it has to be something more.' Kher claims ignorance, but I persist in this line of questioning. 'You see, Ravi Shankar has this theory of music founded on the basic constants of *mo pa ja la.*'

'You better ask Ravi-ji this question,' Kher tells me in an aside.

Extolling the virtues of music, Kher tells me it can even bring the dead back to life. I ask him if he has ever seen this happen. '*Mujhe pata nahin aap kaun si dhara ke prani hain. Main hairan hoon aapse!*' retorts Kher, visibly peeved. I don't know which alien land you belong to. I am shocked! The last straw is when I tell him, with the innocence of a buffoon, that Sufi singers like Nusrat Fateh Ali Khan and Mika Singh sing through their nose. Kher is so outraged that he retorts, '*Kaun hai ye moorakh jo aisi baat keh raha hai?*' Who is this idiot spreading such canards?

Shankar Mahadevan, on the other hand, gets the game straightaway. After some preliminary questions of a somewhat serious nature, Shankar seems to have a fair idea what I'm up to when I ask him, 'What did you do with computers in the gurukul?' He has never been to a gurukul, he corrects me. He is working with a software company. 'Computers and all that is a very rational thought ... in music you have to think chaotic,' I try to argue.

'I do not think rationally. That's why I got into music, where I started thinking irrationally,' Shankar chuckles back.

When I ask him whether he agrees that *sa re ga ma* should be replaced by *mo pa ja la*, he answers, rolling his eyes, 'Great idea. Actually, people should go with fashion, people should go with the new trends.' He is able to play it as wittily as my twisters demand.

There is no one as pompous as the fashion designers, though, who stick their nose in the air the minute I deliberately mispronounce something. I interview J.J. Valaya, Rohit Bal and Manish Arora for the show. Bal is a sport while Valaya and Arora take it stoically. Valaya is least impressed with my knowledge of haute couture, as is Arora. I ask them some regulation questions, like how they bring sex appeal into a dress, how much 'oomph-factor' there is in their clothes, and how important genes are to fashion.

The answers are all clichés. Valaya, for instance, glorifies fashion, saying, 'Fashion can give you confidence, multi-culturality. Oomph is only one element; there are so many languages that fashion speaks.' I tell him I've heard he also makes sofas, and ask how many 'hot cot' he has made in the last year. 'Somebody who has framed your questions needs some knowledge,' he informs me. I spell out what I'm saying. He corrects my diction and goes on to explain what 'haute couture' is all about.

After the lesson is over, our discussion moves to beauty and ugliness. I ask him how important beauty is to fashion. 'One doesn't have to be physically fantastic to be a beautiful person,' he points out.

'So, ugly can be the beauty also?'

He defines beauty in a philosophical way. 'If you are doing great work and touching people's lives, then you are probably more beautiful.'

Valaya can't take it any longer when I ask him why they call him a big gun and whether this sobriquet has anything to do with his arms. 'Is that a serious question, because this is turning out to be a very funny show?' He laughs nervously before swishing out of the room.

Manish Arora also runs short of patience. Among the host of inanities I pillory him with, a sampler: 'Do you like fish fry? Why your clothes are called Fish Fry? Many people say your clothes are non vegetarian. So they don't buy your clothes. What do you think? How many hot cot you have done so far?'

He scratches his balding pate before correcting me. 'No, over all this interview is not really ... It is quite embarrassing. ... I have never given an interview like this with all these questions which are so bizarre and so wrong.' I have bumped into Arora several times after that, and though we exchange civilities, he always maintains a stern demeanour.

My twisted English and equally twisted questions make Rohit Bal laugh, though he tries to answer them seriously. When he tells me attitude is the only thing in fashion, I ask him why people wear clothes at all. Bal gropes for words. 'It is social conditioning,' he explains. It goes on like this, with Bal even trying to correct my English. I am not a good learner. By the end of the interview, he knows he has been taken for a ride on the lines of MTV Bakra.

Shahnaz Husain, the beautician, starts with a strong sales pitch for her products and never deviates. She says she sells civilisation in a jar, so I ask her how big the jar is. 'Whatever I present to the Western world, it has India's 3,000 BC civilisation in it,' she philosophises. At least the tsarina of the jar has some sense of a historical timeline.

If Husain sells civilisation in a beauty jar, Shikha Sharma sells the Ayurvedic concept of healthy eating, cast as a constant tussle between tamasik and sattvik. The cardiologist-turned-dietician fends off my crackers with a broad, toothy smile. She tells me, for instance, that a man becomes what he eats. If I eat chicken, will I become a chicken, I wonder aloud. 'You say you don't believe in medicine. If a patient doesn't take medicine, won't he die?' I ask. 'When did I say medicine isn't required?' she replies, furrowing her brow.

Samantha Kochhar and Javed Habib are two celebrities from the beauty business who are real sports. In fact, Habib gets the game as soon as I ask him if dandruff can be traded like hair. Maybe the wig I am wearing gives me away. He is, after all, a stylist whose fingers converse with hair. When I ask him how many cities he has cut hair in, he says, 'I've even cut hair on the moon.' When the interview ends, he says, *'Enjoy kiya na hum logon ne?'*

'What should one do to stop hair loss? The latest trend is to use goat piss. Do you do that?' The questions I throw at Samantha Kochhar are enough to drive any guest crazy, but she has more mettle than that.

'I wish it was that, but I would suggest that if it goes, it just goes,' says the Delhi-based make-up expert and hair stylist. Perhaps my weird English gives the game away. She has a huge laugh when the interview is over.

Ayan and Aman Ali Khan also have a good laugh when I pronounce jazz as juice and ask them if they've ever attempted a fusion of Indian classical with juice. Testing their general knowledge, I tell them that astronaut Sunita Williams has decided to play the raga Dhani in space. Is it a good raga to play in space? *'Agar Sunita-ji ne select kiya hai toh must be, she must be having some vision,'* the senior sibling opines, all seriousness.

'What is your favourite crime?' gets me a puzzled damn-you look from the gutsy IPS officer (retired) Kiran Bedi.

'It is nothing but a mental illness if a crime becomes someone's favourite,' she tells me. I am lucky enough to get away with questions like 'Why shouldn't the government auction crimes like pick-pocketing?' and probably leave her wondering if I'm nuts.

It is not as easy an undertaking, however, to grill a comedian. Sunil Pal, true to his profession, makes us both laugh in his inimitable style. When asked, for instance, if he makes comedy for man or for animal, the stand-up comedian observes, 'Nahin, abhi tak toh humara desh aur humare kalakar itne advance nahin huye hain ki janwaron ko aap hansa sakein.' No, our country and artistes are not yet so advanced that they can make animals laugh.

I try to unsettle Shiv Khera, but the glib talker that he is, the motivational speaker keeps a cool yet stiff mien throughout the show, delivering a monologue. It is really difficult to look at him without staring awkwardly. I get quite an earful. 'Let me put it this way, Tony. There is no such thing as business motivation. Either you have motivation or you don't have motivation.' Or, 'Winners have the habit of doing things losers don't like to do. The things losers don't like to do are the same things winners don't like to do either, but they do it anyway. Losers don't like to work hard but winners also don't like to work hard either, but they have done it anyway.'

Like millions of my fellow countrymen, cricket is my favourite sport. Tony B would be a no-show if he didn't pull the leg of a few cricketers. I manage to rope in about half a dozen. I ask them all kinds of questions—how spitting on the ball affects the swing, whether they hit a six with one leg or both legs planted, what is more important, muscle or memory, and if they play one-tippa ball, two-tippa ball or surra ball. Batsman Aakash Chopra is one of the cricketers at the receiving end of such googlies. He attempts to answer while trying not to lose his cool. 'Your knowledge of cricket is not something to write home about,' an exhausted Chopra finally tells me.

There are many interviews that Star One and Channel V don't run, in particular those with Mukhtar Abbas Naqvi, Girija

Vyas and M.S. Bitta. Vyas, then the chairperson of the National Commission for Women, is hard to ruffle, even when perhaps she should have been. When I ask her which state a man should go to if he wants to beat his wife, Vyas says with a frown, 'Nowhere.'

Naqvi jumps the gun when I start talking about Kashmir and say, 'People say Article 307 should be scrapped. Do you agree?' Clearly not hearing what I've said, he answers, 'Definitely, it should be done.' When it comes to Nandigram, he denounces the Dalai Lama's 'proposal': 'What happened in Nandigram cannot be undone with such proposals.'

M.S. Bitta confines himself to his pet theme, terrorism. My bouncer, 'Which is the bigger terrorist, the Lashkar-e-Taiba or the Income Tax Department?' leaves him dumbfounded, before he recovers to explain to me the difference between the two.

I wish Channel V and Star One had aired more of these interviews, in order to allow audiences to have a laugh at the expense of some of their political masters. One of the crucial aspects of a healthy democracy is the expressiveness of its comics and the use of humour to question the abuse of power. It defangs the autocrats, so to speak, and makes them lose their shine over a period of time.

## DIABOLICAL FORENSICS

In 2007, we do a story for Star News about how personnel from a forensic laboratory are willing to provide false forensic reports for money. For Rs 2 lakh, one can get a forensic report that allows one to get away with even a heinous crime like murder. For Rs 2 lakh, one can convert death to murder by poisoning. Many of the staff of the Agra-based Forensic Science Laboratory, from the peons to the assistant directors and senior scientists, make an appearance in this story. In typical Hindi-headline fashion, Star titles the report 'Kanoon ke Killer'.

The story is based on the information that reporter Harish Sharma has about goings-on in the lab. He has a breakthrough meeting with Assistant Director Rau Das, head of the ballistic division, at the Agra Fort one evening. Das's peon, Amrit Lal Pushkar, brings him there to strike a deal with Harish, who acts as a decoy customer. Das not only agrees to change a ballistic report to suit his client but also confesses to have similarly bailed out a member of the Delhi Police who had murdered someone in Dadri. He charges Rs 2 lakh for his own services and Rs 50,000 for those of his team members. Scientific Officer Raghavendra Yadav will do the favour for Rs 40,000. For Rs 2 lakh, Das's fellow director Raj Veer Singh agrees to report a deadly poison in the viscera of a dead woman to help implicate an innocent person in a supposed dowry death case.

Star News breaks the story on 9 August 2007. While Das and Singh are dismissed, the rest of the staff get away with lighter punishments. I hear later that Singh has been able to get relief from the Allahabad High Court.

Around the same time, we do a series of stories for Star News in a programme called *Benaqaab*. A lot of these never got the traction they deserve because Star News is a lone Hindi channel, with no supporting English channel or national news presence.

If one can buy a favourable report from the staff of a government forensic lab, one can also buy, with as much ease, weaponry, ammunition and even drugs from none other than the keepers of the law. Guns and contraband seized by the police during an investigation are kept at the Sadar malkhana, within the court premises, while cases are heard. 'Aaj ke Yamraj', which airs on Star News on 11 November 2007, shows the policemen in charge of these storehouses selling seized items to potential criminals. A clerk and a sub-inspector at the Meerut malkhana, and another person in Farrukhabad, sell recovered country-made pistols to Kumar Ashish—one of Cobrapost's star reporters, who poses as a customer—for the paltry sum of Rs 1,000 apiece. A constable at the Kamalganj police station strikes a deal in full sight of a hidden camera to sell heroin worth Rs 1 crore.

'Kinnar' brings to light certain aspects of life within the Indian transgender community that makes a living off dancing and singing. The story exposes a racket run by a few touts and self-styled 'doctors' who operate on some teenagers without their consent, consigning them to a life usually fraught with abuse. The touts establish a relationship with the teenagers and take care of their needs before having them castrated to increase their gang membership.

Another inhuman crime we investigate is child abuse in the form of enforced begging. The street children one often sees asking for money around traffic signals in big cities are victims of state neglect and predatory cartels. According to a National Human Rights Commission report (2017–2018), around 300,000 children across the country are drugged, beaten and forced to beg every day. These numbers have increased as begging has become an Indian industry. Operation Beggar, an investigation we undertake in 2006, narrates the story of such children, including those staying at shelters run by NGOs. We find that children can be traded for money as well.

While looking for such racketeers around night shelters at the Old Delhi railway station, Harish chances upon Raja and gains his confidence. One morning, Raja calls Harish, his would-be client, to the Akshardham temple, where he says he has brought a van-load of children who can be bought for Harish's stated purpose: smuggling gold in Bombay. Raja reveals some of the shocking secrets of his trade: kids are drugged to make them pliant, and if any child proves too stubborn, he or she is killed in the jungle behind Majnu Ka

Tila, and the corpse is disposed of using an ambulance from LNJP Hospital.

Raja even takes the Cobrapost team to the killing spot, where he gives them a demo of how to break a recalcitrant child's neck. Believing this to be a golden opportunity to earn big bucks, he casually remarks that he can arrange kids for his clients from Prayas, an NGO run by Amod Kanth, a former DGP of Goa and Arunachal Pradesh. Raja introduces our reporter to Chandra Shekhar, who works with Prayas's Nabi Kareem shelter. For Rs 20,000, Chandra Shekhar is willing to lend us three kids from Prayas, whom we say we need on 23 September 2006, the day Star News will run the story.

After the broadcast, Chandra Shekhar is arrested, while Raja and his accomplice Rajesh disappear. Chandra Shekhar is given only a two-year sentence. Later, another man involved in the racket will be arrested by the Delhi Police.

Two more stories merit mention, both of which expose the seedy side of religious preachers. One is 'Fatwa'. Broadcast by Star News, the story shows muftis and maulvis issuing religious edicts for money. They decree, for a price, that the following are haraam: buying a double-bed or TV, using a credit card, women wearing jeans, polio drops for children, and what not.

If Muslims have such gurus, Hindus have plenty of godmen happy to earn crores on the sly. Broadcast by IBN-7, our story 'Maya' is a shocker for the millions of followers of Pilot Baba, Vedanti Maharaj, Suryam Namboodiri, Swami Pragyanand, Acharya Pramod, Kireet Maharaj and Pandit Anil Kumar Joshi. These babas have been acting as conduits for money laundering, charging one-third of the total amount laundered as their fee.

During the course of our investigations, we face countless legal challenges, but we survive. Cobrapost provides investigative content to India's top TV channels, from AajTak to Star News, the

CNN-IBN network, Times Now and others. I also observe many of our public interest stories being dropped by the top hierarchy of these channels—how widespread the use of child labour is for picking BT cotton in Gujarat, the deaths caused due to mica dust in several households, and the impact of groundwater pollution, to name a few. I am told that sad stories don't get television ratings and that advertisers don't want their products to be associated with 'suffering and sadness'.

More alarmingly, some of the stories we provide to a particular channel partner end up in the hands of a senior political leader. I learn about this in a rather comical way when a flunky of the politician in question approaches me with great conspiratorial glee, asks if I'm interested in doing a press conference about a political party, and then provides me with the same story that Cobrapost has provided to the channel. This happens a second time, and again, I review the story and pretend that it is not my cup of tea. When the flunky does it a third time, I can no longer tolerate his bullshit and reveal to him that the stories are originally from Cobrapost, and that he had better go and tell his political leader that whoever is passing stories on to him is a rogue editor.

Of course, I know who is passing on the stories. When I raise the issue with the channel editor, he expresses his helplessness, even though he is aware of the breach. He tells me that even the owner of the channel knows what is happening but is helpless, as the rogue editor is a favourite of the political party in question and under no circumstances can the person be read the riot act.

From 2013 onwards, many of India's television channels have become 'saffronised', so to speak. Between 2005 and 2013, most Hindi channels depended on crime, cricket and Bollywood for TRPs. They coarsened the conversation and even peddled superstition as news. But they were wary of doing propaganda for any particular political party. Things change in the year before the

2014 Lok Sabha elections. The English channels join in, too, and propaganda takes over the news. Earlier, TRPs could skew the news one way or another, but they now share this responsibility with the political predilections of the channel owner.

Whether the saffronisation is purely for commercial gain or the result of a combination of commercial interests, fear of the state, TRPs and the personal ideological leanings of channel owners is a question that remains to be answered. Nearly all the national channels of repute are stationed out of Noida in Uttar Pradesh. With all the national TV media houses operating within the UP government's jurisdiction, its capacity for mischief is immense.

The weekly TRP battle has corroded the mental fibre of the editors at these channels. Since 2013, after turning non-profit, we have had more flexibility in how we run our stories. Quite often, we have held press conferences and then amplified our stories through different media platforms.

## DEMOCRACY FOR SALE

'They have told me they will charge Rs 50 lakh. I have spoken to them.'

Dateline: 2 August 2010

Cobrapost goes into hibernation in 2008 and 2009. There are no contracts with any channels, and I don't go looking for them. Instead, I take the time to finish my historical novel, *The Emissary*. In 2010, Rajdeep Sardesai approaches Cobrapost, and we negotiate a small contract with Network18. A few of my former Cobrapost reporters are insistent that I start again, as they are hungry to do some good stories.

Sometime then, Kumar Ashish learns that Rajya Sabha seats are being sold in Jharkhand, and MLAs are looking for buyers of votes. The state sends six members to the Upper House. Kumar Ashish does some groundbreaking work on the story to substantiate the rumours and whispers. We get proof on tape that the Rajya Sabha can be bought.

Two months later, we break the story on CNN-IBN. Aptly named 'Rajya Sabha for Sale', the story shows several legislators agreeing to cast their votes for money. Their fee ranges from Rs 50 lakh to Rs 2 crore. Congress MLA Rajesh Ranjan is an ace broker. He brings three legislators who are willing to barter their votes, to parade them before our reporter at a hotel. He also gets some more legislators on the phone, who agree to cast their votes in favour of the candidate who will pay for them. Ranjan promises to bring eleven Congress MLAs on board with the deal.

Interestingly, this is the year businessman Kanwar Deep Singh is elected. He later changes his allegiance to Mamata Banerjee's Trinamool Congress.

We capture six state legislators on camera, negotiating to sell their votes: Rajesh Ranjan, Sawan Lakda and Yogendra Sao of the Congress; Simon Marandi and Teklal Mahato of the Jharkhand Mukti Morcha (JMM); and Uma Shankar Akela of the BJP.

The story gets nationwide coverage. *Prabhat Khabar*, a prominent daily published from Jharkhand, devotes an entire edition to it, complete with log sheets. But it wrongly credits the story to a reporter who has nothing to do with it. Although the paper carries a corrigendum the next day, after it comes to know of the slip, Ashish still rues their mistake.

The revelations lead to shock and outrage. Shaken, both the Congress and the BJP gun for their members. Strangely, though, the JMM defends its legislators. The Election Commission of

India takes suo moto action and lodges an FIR with the state police. However, the commission spares two of the Congress MLAs. An inquiry follows. In 2013, the Jharkhand High Court steps in, responding to a PIL, and directs the CBI to take over the case. Inevitably, progress in the case has been tardy, with the CBI only chargesheeting five MLAs in 2015.

## SYED'S STORIES

Syed is a reporter who authors some groundbreaking stories for Cobrapost. One of these is 'The Baby Bazar', which is broadcast by IBN7 in 2012. It shows how the staff of government hospitals in Uttar Pradesh, including doctors and nurses, sell babies for adoption. We see in the footage, to our horror, a doctor casually dangling an infant upside down in the air in front of our reporter, his 'potential client'. These babies are sourced from poor parents who do not have the money to afford treatment for the diseases they suffer from.

'My Name is Khan' (15 August 2008) is another story by Syed that stands out. It shows how impossible it is for a Muslim to find rented accommodation in urbane, upscale housing societies in cities like Delhi and Bombay.

Syed has a fecund, indomitable mind and the gumption to take an idea to its logical conclusion. In 2012, while working on another story on the Censor Board, he gets a tip-off. Tapping his sources, he gets through to some tinsel town biggies. A few months later, we have another breaking story. 'The Real Dirty Picture' shows, for the first time, how cinema rides high on black money. Producers like Basu Bhagnani, Anees Bazmi and Anubhav Sinha are shown clamouring for investments of black money in their films. The story spurs the Income Tax Department to action, and they seek out our raw footage. But they soon develop cold feet.

Later, Syed gets a mysterious call from one of the Gulf countries. '*Aap Bambai aaye aapne humare saath chai nahin pee,*' the caller says in a heavy accent. You visited Bombay but left without having a cup of tea with me. Undoubtedly, an indirect threat to let him know he is being watched.

## WASHING DIRTY MONEY

> 'Give whatever you want. Basically, you don't have to show that your money is coming to us. We have this insurance scheme where it will surely be invested.'
> Dateline: 15 March–14 May 2013

One of our most impactful investigations is Operation Red Spider, which exposes nearly three dozen Indian and foreign banks and insurance companies for money laundering. The banks, both private and public, include all the big names: HDFC, ICICI, Axis, the Life Insurance Corporation of India, the State Bank of India.

To get this story, Syed visits more than three hundred bank branches in over a dozen cities all over India. When his sources first suggested to him that there was rampant money laundering going on in Indian banks, we were both rather sceptical. But after receiving specific information about certain banks and managing to corroborate it, it was open season.

Syed's cover story is simple. A politician wants to launder his ill-gotten cash—can the banks help? One might think no banking personnel will interact with an individual after he discloses such intentions, but they all want a piece of the action.

Syed keeps checking in from the field so we knew he is safe. All it will take for him to be compromised is one suspicious banker. On one occasion, he does find himself in a tight spot. When he goes to see an LIC manager to discuss his proposal, coincidentally, the manager brings in a colleague from another LIC branch that Syed had visited a few days earlier. He just about manages to keep his wits about him and talk his way out of the situation without raising suspicion.

Other than these little hiccups, the fieldwork goes smoothly. In fact, Syed internalises his role as a politician's frontman so well that, in his own words, he begins to feel as if he is actually working for a politician, and his only job is to visit banks to see if they can wash his master's illicit money clean.

Many of the bankers and insurers suggest imaginative ways to convert black money into white, in the form of illegal deposits, insurance and investment products. For instance, opening an escrow account is one way to get black money into the regular banking system without the regulatory authorities ever finding out. We discover that:

- One can invest huge amounts of cash in insurance products, gold and other instruments.
- This can be done even without the mandatory PAN card or adhering to the KYC norms laid down by the RBI.
- 'Benami' accounts can also be used to convert black money into white.
- Black money can be channelised into the system using the accounts of other customers, for a fee.

- This can also be done by opening multiple accounts and closing them after the objective has been achieved.
- Bank lockers can be used for the safekeeping of illegitimate cash.
- Black money can also be transferred abroad through NRE (Non-Resident External) or NRO (Non-Resident Ordinary) accounts. Money can be transferred telegraphically or through means beyond the regular banking channels.

We break up the story into four parts. After the first part is released on 15 March 2013, the RBI enters denial mode, declaring that the Indian banking system is foolproof and there are no malpractices by the banks in question. But the regulatory body begins singing a different tune when we release the second part, with an investigation into the banks we have exposed. After we release the last part of the story, the RBI imposes fines on various banks while tightening the KYC norms. Many banks suspend the staff members who were caught on camera. What happens in the wake of Operation Red Spider is unprecedented.

While previous fines levied on banks by the RBI were like feathers falling on knuckles, this time they are significant by Indian standards—as high as Rs 5 crore on certain banks. Many friends have complained to me about the strict KYC norms that banks have begun following from then on. Even the insurance sold by bank employees is better regulated than before. Incidentally, not a single bank even sends us a legal notice. A story of this magnitude in the West would perhaps have led to the closure of several institutions. You can't float around in the branches of Western banks or make cold calls saying that you want to launder a politician's cash. If senior banking staff there were to advise you on how to proceed, and were to go on to narrate in detail how they helped others do so in the past, their banks wouldn't survive the scandal. But here, there is too much importance given to the 'survivability of the system'. Simply put, the banks are too big to fail.

Syed has one legitimate grudge—that the RBI does not raid the lockers of the banks that are exposed. But then, doing so would have been proof of its own failings.

Something else happens with this story. Though I contact many TV channels, all of them refuse to partner with us. Maybe they are concerned about their bottom line, as many of the investigated banks are regular advertisers and sponsors. I personally approach the editors of many TV channels, requesting them to at least cover the Cobrapost press conference. This leads to the Ministry of Information and Broadcasting advising channels not to carry the Cobrapost exposé live. That is when I make up my mind to turn Cobrapost into a non-profit.

The night before we break the story, there is a lot of tension in the office. We are unsure whether we will be able to meet the production deadline for the next day's press conference, but we manage it in the end. I also receive several calls from people who are on my Facebook friends list. Perhaps the story has been leaked. One of them asks me why I've deleted the name of a 'particular bank' from the next day's exposé. Groggily, I tell him that our story has nothing to do with banks at all. When he persists, I am rather curt and tell him that he is being presumptuous in assuming that I would reveal the contents of the next day's story to him, whatever it may be about. But the last thing I want is for a bank to get a temporary stay order from a court and spoil months of effort.

Red Spider brings Cobrapost recognition from Transparency International. The story is ranked second best at the One World Media Awards.

# THE MONSTER CALLED SOCIAL MEDIA

'Nobody even among the experts can find it out on Google ... I have put in place proxy codes ... so when we are working the location of the codes keeps on changing.'
Dateline: 29 November 2013

Our lives are driven by technology in one way or the other. But it is a double-edged sword—there's always a downside. These days, most of us communicate with the world beyond our immediate family via Facebook, Twitter, Instagram, WhatsApp and other widely available tools. More than 16 per cent of India's population is hooked to social media. According to one estimate, WhatsApp has more than 250 million active users in a month in India.

Unfortunately, these instant messaging tools are being used to spread rumours and disaffection. Between 2018 and 2019, there were seventeen cases of lynching across India, and in all the documented cases, WhatsApp was used to spread the rumours that led to them. As in Kasganj, in January 2018, social media is capable of causing civil strife and spreading hatred to devastating effect.

Syed sees this coming in 2013, a time when many leaders and celebs are beginning to enjoy a huge following on their social media accounts. Syed thinks there might be something amiss, and speaks to some techies. He learns that, apparently, one can have as many likes or followers on their Twitter or Facebook accounts as money can buy. Anything can be cooked and served on social media. The more he delves into the issue, the seamier this side of social media appears. About a fortnight into his investigation, Syed tells me that it would be a good idea to get a few IT companies to do some negative or defamatory propaganda—terms such as 'trolling' are yet to arrive—to get to the real crux of the story. I promptly tell him to instruct them to target me in the negative campaign. As he meets the owners or senior officials of various IT companies, the names of the leaders and political parties they work for begin to emerge.

Some months down the line, we break the story. Titled Operation Blue Virus, it lays bare some stark truths about social media—likes can be bought and so can followers; you can sway public opinion in your favour or against your opponents to win an election. The investigation demonstrates clearly how IT companies across the country use social media platforms to help politicians artificially boost their popularity and malign their opponents. Cobrapost uncovers two dozen such companies, which are involved in running this shady business of online reputation management.

Posing as a campaigner, Syed approaches companies with a proposal: Neta-ji, his boss, wants to launch an image-building exercise on social media before the upcoming assembly elections. Simultaneously, the reputation of this fictitious neta's opponent has to be destroyed with negative publicity, to help Neta-ji win the assembly election with a handsome margin, and also his party president's trust, to pave the way for a Lok Sabha ticket in 2014, and then a Cabinet berth. Money is not a constraint.

The companies scramble to present to us their most lucrative options, including the generation of fake news, fake fan sites, positive and negative comments. They also offer to use offshore IPs and servers to avoid any tracing of the content's source, and say they can hack into the computers of different individuals for posting defamatory content, using their IPs.

They go so far as to say that they will use an Internet-based messaging system to circumvent TRAI regulations on mass SMS. They can do this using short codes instead of actual phone numbers to mask the identity of the sender. Moreover, they will accept payments only in cash, to avoid a paper trail and ensure that no connection is established between them and the client.

Booth-wise demographics of the electorate are available for the asking, and you can also stop people from voting against you by persuading them to stay at home on election day by spreading rumours through the company. And all this can be done without leaving any footprints by using proxy codes, offshore IPs and servers.

One IT professional named Bipin Pathare is the craftiest and most ruthless of the lot. He is happy to provide booth-wise voter demographics to help with booth management but also to detonate a bomb or spread rumours of a riot, forcing Muslim voters to remain indoors on polling day and leaving ample scope for bogus voting.

Operation Blue Virus gets nationwide coverage in the media, and *Outlook* magazine makes it its cover story. IPS officer Amitabh Thakur lodges an FIR in Lucknow against all twenty-four IT companies that the story has exposed, but the case doesn't go anywhere.

## THE STALKERS

Sometime in 2013, a source comes to meet me at the office of one of my lawyers. He provides us with a dump of audio recordings that contain conversations between Amit Shah, who is the home minister in Gujarat, and a police officer.

The story that comes out of this—'The Stalkers'—uncovers the obsession of a mighty politician from Gujarat, and his use of state police and intelligence apparatus to prey upon a young, Bangalore-based female professional. Released on 15 November 2013, the story is done in partnership with Gulail, a website started by Ashish Khetan, one of India's finest investigative journalists. The report shows how the three key wings of the Gujarat Police—the State Intelligence Bureau, or CID Intelligence, the Crime Branch and the Anti-Terrorist Squad—secretly trailed the woman to record private moments, personal conversations and daily movements, and then reported them back to Amit Shah. This spying operation was conducted at the behest of one 'saheb' back in August 2009.

The story is based on more than 250 audio tapes of conversations between Gujarat IPS officer G.L. Singhal and Amit Shah. The tapes are part of Singhal's deposition before the CBI, which is probing his role in the Ishrat Jahan fake encounter case. Singhal was then the superintendent of police with the Anti-Terrorist Squad, and was close to Shah.

As soon as our story is released, the BJP comes out with a letter from the girl's family, apparently claiming that the surveillance was done at their request, for her own good. All this to protect Narendra Modi, who has been declared the party's prime ministerial candidate in September 2013. In fact, the Cobrapost story never connects 'saheb' to Modi; it is the BJP press conference that does so. An inquiry commission is set up by the state government to investigate what comes to be known as 'Snoopgate'. But the Gujarat High Court will disband the commission in October 2014, following a petition by the father of the woman in question.

## THE DIRTY ELEVEN

'You tell me something ... after all, we have to fight elections that are so expensive.'

Dateline: 12 December 2013

Following numerous tips, Kumar Ashish has another scoop. Again, parliamentarians—eleven of them—are exposed. For this operation, Ashish poses as a representative of a fictional multinational corporation based in Queensland, Australia, complete with a website, brochure and company profile. Our fictional entity, Mediterranean Oil Inc., is in the business of oil exploration and owns rigs worldwide. The company wants to bid for rigging rights in India's northeast. The proposed project is pegged at Rs 1,000 crore. Ashish's onerous task is to get as many MPs as possible to lobby with the Ministry of Petroleum on behalf of our company.

The MPs quote fees ranging from Rs 50,000 to Rs 50 lakh. The corruption cuts across party lines, with MPs from Congress, BJP, BSP, JDU and AIADMK agreeing to write recommendatory letters to the Ministry of Petroleum. Smelling money, none of them has bothered to check the company's antecedents. Six of them deliver to us the promised letters. BJP MP Lalu Bhai Patel not only writes a letter but also agrees to lobby for the company. He demands Rs 50,000 and is duly paid. JDU MP Maheshwar Hazari promises to rope in five MPs—for Rs 5 lakh a pop. Khiladi Lal Bairwa, a Congress MP from Rajasthan, is the most colourful of the lot. Initially he is suspicious and says, 'There's something off … this is like the Coal (gate) affair.' But he too agrees—at the price of Rs 50 lakh. He invites the reporter to his Jaipur residence, telling him to bring the 'material' there. Vikrambhai Arjanbhai, a fellow party man, prefers that an angadia deliver the fee.

Operation Falcon Claw does not stir much dust. Stung by many such scandals, Parliament sits nonplussed. Political parties do their bit by issuing show cause notices to their members.

The bottom line is that there are MPs willing to lobby and write letters for a multinational in return for cash. Who knows how much of this 'lobbying' has happened in the past, and how much more awaits, especially in the absence of any safeguards to ensure that it doesn't happen again? The more I think India has changed, the more I feel things remain the same. Especially among our hardboiled politicos—an incorrigible breed.

## NERO FIDDLED, DELHI BURNED

'He told me, and gave me in writing, that Indira Gandhi's murder is big enough an event. Why should I make it even bigger by opening fire.'

Dateline: 22 April 2014

The October morning on which Prime Minister Indira Gandhi was assassinated by her Sikh security guards opened what would forever remain as one of the darkest chapters in the history of independent India. The following three days were marked by murder and mayhem, as frenzied mobs went about maiming and killing Sikhs, raping women, looting, pillaging and burning homes and businesses. The madness left more than eight thousand Sikhs dead in forty cities across the country. Delhi alone accounted for about three thousand killings. Vengeance was extracted on an entire community for the cowardly act that two of their tribe had committed.

In 2014, three decades and at least half-a-dozen commissions of inquiries later, justice remained elusive. This is often the case in incidents where the state is complicit, first in instigating and fomenting communal frenzy and then in not allowing the law and order machinery to act. The Delhi anti-Sikh riots are a classic case of the state choosing to allow a pogrom to take place.

We revisit the horror of those three days with 'Chapter 84'. Our investigation shows how the Delhi Police failed, and how and why the top brass turned a Nelson's eye to what was happening around them. The confessions of the eight police officers that our reporter Asit Dixit leads us to, help us reach some heinous conclusions, including the fact that an undercurrent of anti-Sikh sentiment was at work in the police force, reflected in its members becoming mute witnesses to rioting and arson, even encouraging the rioters at times. Senior officers had refused to act on repeated warnings of an impending communal flare-up in their respective areas. Only 2 per cent of messages to the control room were recorded. Senior officers changed logbooks to cover up their inertia.

The force was directed to not act against rioters; in other words, to give them a free hand. Many senior officers didn't let subordinates fire on murderous rioters. The police did not register FIRs, and when they did so, they clubbed different cases into one FIR.

Shoorveer Singh Tyagi, then the station house officer (SHO) at Kalyanpuri, makes a significant confession. Implicating then commissioner S.C. Tandon, he says, 'So, knowingly or unknowingly, he was under the influence of the government. He mismanaged in the beginning and in the first two days the situation went out of control.' Ironically, Tyagi was himself accused of disarming Sikhs and forcing them out of a gurdwara in his area. When Tyagi did a disappearing act, the rioters swooped in on the Sikhs, killing five hundred of them.

Another senior officer is put in the dock by one of his subordinates. Rohtas Singh, then the SHO of Delhi Cantonment, blames his boss Chandra Prakash, then deputy commissioner of police, for not allowing him to open fire on rioters. The story is widely covered by the mainstream media, resulting in the political class resuming its blame game for such acts of omission and commission. Chandra Prakash files a case against us, which we win in 2020.

The 1984 cases are still pending in the courts, moving at the usual snail's pace of Indian jurisprudence.

## A SHAKY AADHAR

A story by my colleague Md Hizbollah, known amongst friends as Hizbul, shows how the government machinery tackles corruption. The story, published on 24 March 2014, demonstrates the weaknesses in Aadhaar, the pet project of the UPA government. Hizbul shows how easy it is for any individual to get an Aadhaar made in his name and claim benefits as a bona fide citizen of this country.

Hizbul covers about a dozen Aadhaar centres across Delhi-NCR, Haryana and Madhya Pradesh. All the officials in charge of these centres are willing to issue Aadhaar cards to even Pakistani and Nepali nationals without any relevant documents. They agree to provide identity and other necessary documents required for such clients, who either do not have any proof of identity or are not of Indian origin. Their fee ranges between Rs 250 and Rs 1,000. Ironically, all these centres are functioning out of government-office premises.

Two weak links in the Aadhaar programme emerge from the story. One, anybody can get an Aadhaar with just a declaration from a local legislator or councillor. Two, all the centres are run by private individuals, who are employed for a pittance and have no accountability. Apart from our website, the story is published by the *Times of India*. The BJP even makes it a poll issue in Karnataka.

The story is path-breaking, in the sense that the media takes notice of the loopholes of this government enterprise, and begins to scrutinise it more closely. The Anti-Corruption Bureau (ACB) lodges an FIR against individuals who are falsifying Aadhar records. The ACB also seeks footage of the investigation.

Six years have passed since, but the authorities are yet to record the statements of those involved in the racket, let alone prosecute them. They will, though, ask Hizbul to appear before them time and again. Last I heard, they had decided to file a civil suit against the racketeers—they cannot be prosecuted under anti-corruption laws as they are not government employees.

## THE COST OF AN EXPOSÉ

In 2014, the ruling Akhilesh Yadav government throws open recruitment for 3,000 village development officers. There is to be a written examination and interviews for each vacancy. But it is all a sham, as these vacancies are actually for sale. The asking price for each is between Rs 8 and Rs 13 lakh. Hizbul meets a dozen Samajwadi Party MLAs and leaders, who are part of the government in some capacity or the other or are closely linked to the top decision-makers. During the course of his investigation, Hizbul goes to Moradabad to meet an influential man who is closely related to the Samajwadi Party leadership. However, the interview does not yield any evidence, as both pieces of equipment he carries to tape it go caput, perhaps because of a jammer. We break the story on 9 May 2014.

Hizbul uncovers another story, a huge land-allotment scam in Bhopal. The Madhya Pradesh government has allotted prime plots here to 150 judicial officers and 300 journalists, among others, almost free. Among the beneficiaries are the likes of special investigation team chief for the Vyapam scam, Chandresh Bhushan, and Madhya Pradesh High Court judge Deepak Verma, who will later become a Supreme Court judge. The story, titled 'Law of the Land', is published by *Caravan* on 1 June 2016. One of the journalist beneficiaries of the government's largesse is a close friend of Hizbul. After the story is published, his friend cuts all ties with him. Such are the wages of our profession.

## UP IN THE AIR

'Up in the Air' by Hizbul is about how politicians of all hues use private charter planes to address public rallies during elections. The high-flyers include Rahul Gandhi, Rajnath Singh, L.K. Advani, Sharad Pawar, Sushma Swaraj and Pranab Mukherjee. Sonia Gandhi may have asked her party leaders to fly economy class, but we find members of the Congress breaking her code on more than one occasion. These charters are run by corporate houses, and the story makes it abundantly clear who oils the wheels of our political class and whose interests this class serves.

There are other politicians who use these private charters. Among them are then BJP president Nitin Gadkari, Praful Patel, Veerappa Moily, Shivraj Singh Chouhan, Raman Singh, Parkash Singh Badal, Mayawati, Kiran Kumar Reddy, B.S. Yeddyurappa, Jagdish Shettar, Sadanand Gowda and Jyotiraditya Scindia.

Before the elections, all political parties are required to notify the Election Commission about their star campaigners. After the polls, when political parties submit their expenses to the Election

Commission, they also have to provide the travel details of these campaigners, including whether they travelled by chartered flights or other means. The violations, however, have become so routine that they are happening in broad daylight.

The story underscores how a seemingly innocuous Act like the RTI can aid citizens, not just journalists, in seeking accountability from the highest echelons of the government. Most of the information we gather, including incriminating documents from the Directorate General of Civil Aviation, the Airport Authority of India and a number of private airway companies, such as Aerotech Aviation India Pvt. Ltd and Turbo Aviation Pvt. Ltd, are mostly secured through RTI applications.

The RTI is one of the most powerful weapons citizens have access to in a democracy to keep a check on the powers that be. Without it, it would be only too easy for the country to transform into an oligarchy, where no politician can ever be held accountable for the misuse of public funds and resources. The manner in which the BJP has succeeded in diluting the provisions of the Act is a matter of grave concern.

# OPERATION R:

## THE ASSASSINATION GAMES

It is a love affair of nearly two years. The comic that I produce with Neelabh Banerjee is called *The Adventures of Rhea: The Cobrapost Affair*. It starts off as a fun thing in my head. My mind is easily bored and constantly seeks new challenges. As a kid, I was besotted with the Tintin and Asterix comics, and now I want to recreate that world, complete with the Hergé style of drawing, in today's context.

Writing the story and the panels is perhaps the easy part; initially, I struggle to figure out how to proceed with the drawings. I try out a lot of artists. But line drawing, the Hergé way, is a unique gift and doesn't come easily. I even try shooting in public places with models and then converting these photographs to line drawings to get a more realistic feel, but it doesn't work at all. And the costs keep mounting. Then the brilliant Neelabh comes into the picture. We find that we share a common vision and so we dive into it. It is he who finally brings the idea to life.

We release the comic in an unusual way. I announce a Cobrapost press conference. Our conferences are always well attended.

The press release goes something like this:

> In a covert operation, Cobrapost reveals an insidious nexus between an international terrorist group linked to the ISI and the Taliban who kidnapped foreign officials in India after faking their murders. In the murky maelstrom of terror, Cobrapost reporter Rhea Baughman blows the lid off this miasmatic whirlpool of terrorists and drug dealers operating from the heart of New Delhi even as the Intelligence Bureau and the National Investigative Agency slumbered over various leads to this terrifying plot that Cobrapost sniffed and followed down to its end. The CIA, Mossad, MI6 and the Canadian and Australian intelligence bureaus then botched up an operation to apprehend the terrorist, shooting at each other. The terror group used the Delhi Golf Course as a hub for clandestine meetings. CCTV footage even shows some of them planning their deadly plots while playing golf.
>
> The story throws up many deadly questions: why did the Intelligence Bureau (IB) and Research and Analysis Wing (RAW) not reveal the emergency situation to the National Security Advisor (NSA) initially? Was it because of an internal turf tussle between the two agencies? Why was the NSA kept out of the loop both by the RAW and the IB? Did the PMO officials follow the constitution of India and the laws of the land in dealing

with the situation after it came to their notice? How much ransom was paid? Did anybody get a commission? Did Delhi Police play a dodgy role? Did the CIA manipulate the situation? Were soldiers of the US's Delta Force stationed at a Chhatarpur farm house unknown to the Indian authorities? Is an Afghan minister laundering drug money in Delhi using real estate?

The release is sent out a day before the press conference, and as it reaches journalists, all hell breaks loose. I am inundated with calls from reporters who want to preview the story before the conference! I even receive calls from the *Washington Post* and the *New York Times*, as the story seems to involve intelligence agencies from around the globe. There are calls from highly placed officers in the Intelligence Bureau too, who are keen to know more. I stick to my line—insisting that though I have provided a teaser, it would be better for them to come and attend the press conference and view the documents and video before they write anything about the story.

Almost everyone agrees, except for a few Hindi dailies, which translate the whole press release and run it on their front pages as a big scoop.

As I start addressing the jam-packed press conference, and the real story unfolds, there is stunned silence. For a while, it appears that no one can believe that it has all been a prank. I spot a few of my friends in the media grinning away, but they are few and far between. The majority are unable to link Cobrapost's serious, scam-busting image with a prank. Anticipating this, I've even kept Holi colours in a container for people to throw at me in case they feel offended.

It was good of Karthika, my editor at HarperCollins, to have played along with a release like that. In today's age of hyper media, perhaps no publisher would dare. So much has changed in these last few years.

# LOVE JIHAD DECODED

'I'm like that since my childhood. I have cases pending against me since long ... in 1996–97 when we used to kill Muslims we used to roam around at nights, hunting them down.'

Dateline: 4 October 2015

Love Jihad. The term was floated nearly a decade ago in Kerala and Karnataka, where it was alleged that Muslim men were wooing Hindu women and converting them to Islam. Conversion via love jihad has been a sore point with the Sangh Parivar since then. Although there is little truth to this bogey, the Bajrang Dal, Vishva Hindu Parishad, Durga Vahini, RSS and BJP have made love jihad a cause célèbre in their communal agenda to rally Hindus. It has also consistently brought the BJP rich electoral dividends in recent times.

The notion gained currency during and after the communal riots in Muzaffarnagar in 2013, in which Muslims were targeted. Hundreds lost their lives, homes and hearths, and many women were raped. I saw love jihad becoming a recurrent theme in TV debates and news stories about Muslim men, who were charged with raping and forcibly converting the women they had fallen in love with.

Is there any truth in these reports, or are they just more fodder for polarisation?

The investigative website Gulail and Cobrapost team up once again to investigate the issue. Shazia Nigar of Gulail meets some prominent leaders of the Sangh brotherhood—Sangeet Som and Sanjeev Balian, among others—who are associated with the anti-love jihad campaign to bring Hindu women back to the Hindu fold. As she speaks to them at length in Uttar Pradesh, Karnataka and Kerala, it becomes clear that there is little truth in the Sangh brotherhood's scaremongering claims.

At the same time, the Cobrapost team investigates some cases in Uttar Pradesh of Muslim men accused of raping Hindu women in the name of love. One such accusation is against a man named Abdul Kalam. The investigating officer at the Meerapur police station tells Cobrapost that it is a made-up case. It takes many days for our team to locate the woman in question. When we do, it turns out to be a false lead. Some days later, however, we get a call from the woman. She knows we are trying to trace her and tells us not to look for her anymore. She is married, but her husband is a drug addict and is of no use to her. She has entered into a relationship with Kalam on her own. Love jihad has nothing to do with it. Our team then meets her mother-in-law and son. The mother-in-law has the same story to narrate. Another such case has been registered at Kharkhoda police station, and here, too, the investigating officer punches a hole in the spectre of love jihad.

Operation Juliet, as we name this investigation, shows clinching evidence in the form of confessions by the all-important leaders of the campaign. The Hindu fanatics who are interviewed report adopting certain tactics to rescue the so-called love jihad victims. Chief amongst these is the slapping of fake rape and kidnapping cases on Muslim youth who marry Hindu women. They admit to implicating Muslim men by portraying women as minors, with the help of fake documents. Often, they use coercion, emotional blackmail and violence to force women to leave their Muslim husbands. They also use drugs on love jihad 'victims' to induce temporary amnesia and wean them away from interfaith marriages.

We get Balian and Umesh Malik to confess to their roles in the Muzaffarnagar riots while Shiv Kumar of the Krishna Sena admits to having been a Hindu terrorist whose job was to kill people from minority communities.

## 'WHO KILLED THEM IF THEY DIDN'T?'

Operation Black Rain is one of Cobrapost's stories that I am most proud of.

Between 1996 and 2000, Bihar witnessed a series of attacks on poor Dalits, including women, children and even unborn babies. The Ranveer Sena, a dreaded militia of the Bhumihar landlords, butchered about three hundred Dalits at Sarthua, Bathani Tola, Laxmanpur-Bathe, Shankar Bigha, Miyanpur, Ikwari and other places during this period. The most horrific incident took place on a cold December night in 1997 at Laxmanpur-Bathe, where the murderous sena killed fifty-eight unarmed Dalits, including women and children, in cold blood, using automatic weapons.

The Rashtriya Janata Dal government instituted a commission of inquiry headed by Justice Amir Das following the massacre. However, after a regime change, the commission was disbanded in 2006, before it could submit its report, by the Janata Dal (United)–BJP alliance government headed by Nitish Kumar. The state and the nation collectively forgot about the massacres for the next ten years.

In October 2013, the country was jolted out of its stupor when the Patna High Court acquitted twenty-five Ranveer Sena men of murder charges, citing lack of evidence. In January 2015, the Patna High Court acquitted the twenty-four Ranveer Sena men accused of the Shankar Bigha massacre on similar grounds. It was easy to spot a pattern in the dispensation of justice.

The question echoed across the country: who killed those Dalits if the Ranveer Sena didn't? One person who thought there was more to the story was our ace reporter Kumar Ashish. He was sure there was something amiss. It didn't take him long to query his sources, and in a matter of days, he was crisscrossing the killing fields of Bihar, interviewing the surviving victims of the massacres at Shankar Bigha, Bathani Tola, Laxmanpur-Bathe, Miyanpur, and anyone else who could lead him to the perpetrators.

At Bathani Tola, he met a victim who had survived a massacre in which the Ranveer Sena killed twenty-one Dalit and Muslim farmhands on 21 July 1996. She showed him the stump of a hand that had been chopped off by an attacker and said matter-of-factly, 'Don't I know who chopped my hand? Who would know it if I don't?'

Soon, posing as a film-maker working on a film on the Ranveer Sena, Ashish interviewed Chandkeshwar alias Chandreshwar, Pramod Singh, Bhola Singh Rai, Arvind Kumar Singh, Siddhnath Singh and Ravindra Chaudhry. All of them, except Ravindra Chaudhry, had been accused in the Laxmanpur-Bathe massacre. Chandkeshwar and Pramod Singh had been set free by the Patna High Court, and Bhola Singh, Arvind Kumar Singh and Siddhnath Singh were let off the hook by lower courts. Bhola Singh was still wanted by the Bihar Police, and was holed up in the steel city of Tata Nagar in Jharkhand.

The men Ashish interviewed revealed not only how they planned and carried out killings on such a scale, with the precision and ruthlessness of a war machine, but also candidly admitted to having been trained, armed and financed by some well-known politicians.

Ashish's breakthrough came when his source led him to Bhola Singh, in his hideout in Jamshedpur, and he openly admitted that Laxmanpur-Bathe was the most 'important' massacre conducted by his organisation, the Ranveer Sena: *'Saath pachas ko wahi par mara tha Laxmanpur-Bathe mein.*' We killed about fifty–sixty people then and there in Laxmanpur-Bathe.

Bhola Singh recounted the assault on Laxmanpur-Bathe without any sign of remorse: 'We worked out a plan and attacked while everyone was asleep. Everyone was caught by surprise and killed, and we suffered no casualties.'

The men gave information about who financed them and trained them, who helped them procure lethal weapons (AK-47s, LMGs, semi-automatics and Mousers), and who provided them with political support. The names of prominent politicians—former prime minister Chandra Shekhar, Yashwant Sinha, Anand Mohan Singh and Arun Kumar—figured in these confessions.

Chandkeshwar turned out to be a particularly cold-blooded killer. 'As the clock struck three, our sena began shooting. Three in the afternoon is when the massacre happened, that too, near a police chowki.' He also provided a headcount: 'Some of the bodies from the assault had been cleared out, but still there were twenty-two bodies on the spot … yes, twenty-two corpses lying around.' He said the massacre was executed at the behest of a man named Gupteshwar Singh from Khandau village. Chandkeshwar even confessed to beheading five men so he wouldn't have to waste expensive bullets on them.

One of the most remarkable things about these murderers was that none of them showed an iota of remorse for what they had done. They were more upset about the fact that their deeds had gone unnoticed by their own community.

One of these fugitives was Upendra Magiha, the Ranveer Sena's second-in-command after its founder, Barmeshwar Mukhiya, who is alleged to have killed about one hundred Dalits. Ashish walked ten kilometres to meet Magiha at his nondescript mud hideout, but Magiha turned him away. The exposé would have been much more sensational, perhaps, if he could have been persuaded to talk.

Nevertheless, the story's impact was stunning. Many Dalit organisations hit the streets to demand justice, while the politicians, as usual, went into denial. If there is one story that really needed a suo moto intervention by the highest judiciary, it was Operation Black Rain, but this did not happen.

## BREAKING THE RSS STORY

> 'You know what happened that day in Delhi when I was there to receive those girls. All the people from our organization reached there. About 200 workers reached there (at the railway station) and asked me to breathe easy. They will take care of everything, they told me.'
>
> Dateline: 29 July 2016

Sometime in August 2015, Syed gets a tip-off about the trafficking of a group of tribal girls from Assam. It appears that though the girls were de-boarded at the New Delhi railway station by various government agencies, they were mysteriously handed back to their handlers to be taken to an unknown destination. Syed begins to follow the feeble lead he has from a station tea stall. But investigators, be it law enforcement agencies or journalists, often have to build a case from scratch. The biggest challenge is to find out who had the power to force the Delhi Police to return those thirty-one girls into the custody of their handlers. Where were the girls taken? For what purpose?

Syed's inquiries with the railways yield another small piece of information—the girls were not sent to their destination the same day; they stayed overnight, somewhere near Nigambodh Ghat, a

Hindu crematorium. After scouring the area surrounding the ghat for many days, Syed goes back to the railway station. Finally, one of the bus drivers there tells him that Delhi Police personnel had herded the girls into a bus that took them to some 'Swamy' ashram near Nigambodh Ghat. This breakthrough leads him to the Swami Narayan Mandir where the thirty-one girls spent the night, and from which twenty were sent onwards to an RSS school in Valsad, Gujarat, and the rest to Patiala in Punjab. The pieces fall into place one by one. After Syed meets the parents of the girls in Assam, we have a big story in hand.

Syed has a close shave while returning from Valsad, when he finds his car being trailed by the Gujarat Police. It turns out that the head of the school, whom Syed could not meet, has a brother serving in the Gujarat Police. Syed also faces a daunting challenge in Patiala, as the school where the eleven Assamese girls had been taken to, has been relocated. Thanks to a spirited employee of the India Post, he reaches the right address.

Operation Shuddhikaran shows how the RSS, through its well-entrenched network of pracharaks across the country, is coaxing poor parents to give away their children to be converted to Hinduism and brainwashed into the Sangh school of thought.

Coincidently, *Outlook* comes out with a similar story around the same time. Journalist Neha Dixit does a lot of field work and teams up with *Outlook* for its publication.

## OPERATION JANMABHOOMI

The demolition of the Babri Masjid in Ayodhya on 6 December 1992 tested India's resilience as a democracy; most would agree it shredded it to pieces. Watching the three domes of the mosque falling one by one as Uma Bharti exhorted the multitudes of Hindu fanatics with the war cry '*Ek dhakka aur do Babri Masjid tod do*' (Give it one more shove, bring the Babri Masjid down), was an apocalyptic moment for the nation. As the building turned into rubble, we saw Bharti hug Murli Manohar Joshi in jubilation while L.K. Advani rejoiced. He was, after all, the architect of the movement.

The Narasimha Rao government at the Centre ordered a judicial inquiry. The Liberhan Commission took seventeen long years to submit its findings, finally doing so in 2009. The CBI framed charges against forty-nine individuals, including Advani, Joshi, Uma Bharti, Vinay Katiyar and Ashok Singhal.

More than two and half decades later, none of the accused has been convicted. Some of them are dead, as are the original plaintiffs and defendants of the dispute. All these years, senior leaders of the Sangh Parivar have claimed that they had nothing to do with the conspiracy to tear the mosque, and the country, apart. What happened that day was 'spontaneous', they say.

Ashish kept a close watch on the developments. He was the last person to buy such arguments from politicians. To a logical mind, it was clear that sabotage of this scale could not be done by an unruly mob. Such acts need logistical support, which calls for planning and preparation. The Liberhan Commission had already highlighted the conspiracy angle in its 2009 report. In 2011, the Supreme Court stayed the ruling of the Allahabad High Court's Lucknow bench, partitioning the disputed land between the UP Sunni Central Waqf Board, the Nirmohi Akhara and Ram Lalla. The ball was in the apex court's court, and the accused were still being tried in the UP courts.

Finally, in May 2017, the special court framed charges under Section 120 B (criminal conspiracy) of the Indian Penal Code, against Advani, Joshi and Bharti along with former MP Vinay

Katiyar and Vishva Hindu Parishad leaders Vishnu Hari Dalmia and Sadhvi Ritambhara. In April, the Supreme Court used its extraordinary constitutional powers under Article 142 to overrule the Allahabad High Court judgment, which in 2010 upheld a CBI special court's 2001 decision to drop conspiracy charges against Advani and the others. The court clearly declared the demolition illegal and recognised the conspiratorial nature of the events that had been given the garb of spontaneity. Our story provided a lot of evidence here.

In 2014, Ashish thought it was time the conspiracy was investigated. He interviewed twenty-three of the leaders at the forefront of the Ram Janmabhoomi movement, who were involved in the demolition of the Babri Masjid, either as conspirators or as executors of the conspiracy to bring down the disputed structure. Posing as an author researching a book on the movement, Ashish spoke to fifteen of the people indicted by the Liberhan Commission and nineteen of those named in the CBI chargesheet. Some faced trial in the CBI court, either as executors or conspirators. Ashish visited Ayodhya, Faizabad, Tanda, Lucknow, Gorakhpur, Mathura and Moradabad in Uttar Pradesh, Jaipur in Rajasthan, Aurangabad and Bombay in Maharashtra, and Gwalior in Madhya Pradesh to interview these principal actors behind the demolition.

He met Kamlesh Kumar, who was among the accused in the case. The Ayodhya resident lived in the immediate vicinity of the mosque, and told Ashish that he had nothing to do with its demolition. He claimed it was a namesake who was involved, and the police had found it convenient to frame him. Two more people claimed to have been framed in the same manner by the CBI. Ashish's visits to East Delhi and Rajasthan drew a blank—the accused existed only on the CBI chargesheet.

The conspiracy clearly required orchestration and execution on many levels. Some of the people involved were laymen of the calibre of the cadre, pawns in the game, such as Dharmendra Singh Gurjar of the Bajrang Dal. He understood the bigger picture a tad too late: 'Our country keeps being fooled—the whole exercise was a matter of making a fool out of people. I was young and in the throes of youth, a kind of fervent madness that eventually passed. People used us, then discarded us.'

Some were mid-level operators. For instance, leaders like Ramji Gupta, who was put in charge of the Laxman Sena, claimed that the army had a simple brief: Once they heard the war cry *'Jai Sheshavatar'*, they were to launch the attack using the crowds as cover, and not stop till they finished the job.

Some powerful people, like the sitting chief minister of UP, Kalyan Singh, had foreknowledge of the events. Mahant Ram Vilas Vedanti quite categorically claimed to have conveyed a message to Singh the night before: 'On the night of December 5, Kalyan Singh was sent the news, told that if necessary the structure would be felled, and that he could decide what to do accordingly.' Beyond this, Sakshi Maharaj also claimed to have given Kalyan Singh a minute-by-minute account of the developments.

Maharaj, in his bid to cover his tracks, put the blame for the killings squarely on Ashok Singhal, saying: 'Right in front of me, Ashok Singhal said to Vamdev Maharaj, "If some people don't die, this movement will not gain momentum." Vamdev Maharaj said if children died it would be disastrous ... (Singhal) said, 'Maharaj, until there are deaths, nothing will happen—only then will it get the fillip it needs.'

Uma Bharti similarly implicated Vinay Katiyar for the killing of the Kothari brothers on 30 October 1990: 'The deaths were because of a mistake Vinay made. Not a mistake, the stampede began in a narrow alley. By mistake, I mean he ran away, abandoning the group.'

It took Ashish almost one and a half years to wrap up his investigation and the intense series of meetings with the perpetrators and conspirators of the crime. We broke the story on 1 July 2016, showing the world for the first time how the conspiracy had been hatched and by whom, and how it had been executed. The story was christened after the codename the conspirators had given to their mission—Operation Janmabhoomi.

The report exposed the callous and murderous face of the Hindutva brigade. Our story brought to light certain facts:

- The appearance of Ram Lalla in Ayodhya in 1949 was not the result of divine intervention.
- Vishva Hindu Parishad leader Ashok Singhal played a central role in the conspiracy.
- The Bajrang Dal executed the conspiracy.
- Training camps, focussed on how to bring down the structure, were organised in Sarkhej, Gujarat.
- The jawans of the Provincial Armed Constabulary of Uttar Pradesh extended help to the demolition men.
- All the logistics were in place before D-Day.
- The Kothari brothers were used as sacrificial goats at the altar of the Ram Janmabhoomi movement.

During the course of our investigation, Ramesh Pratap Singh, one of the executioners of the conspiracy, became suspicious after Ashish taped their conversation. He called Ashish over to a construction site among acres of agricultural land close to a village in Basti. Ashish saw around fifteen people having alcohol inside the premises. Some were Muslims, who dropped an unmistakable hint to him, to get out of there when Singh excused himself to fetch something. Ashish made himself scarce without wasting a moment.

The demolition changed India's social and political landscape forever. On that day, some journalists tasted first-hand how

Hindutva would unfold, when they were manhandled and beaten mercilessly by Hindu fanatics in the presence of the top leadership of the RSS and the BJP.

Despite crucial details emerging during the case, I have now lost all hope of our story being vindicated. The last nail in the coffin was the September 2020 judgement of the special CBI Court in Lucknow, which acquitted all the thirty-two accused, including erstwhile veteran BJP (and Sangh Parivar) leaders L.K. Advani, Murli Manohar Joshi and Uma Bharti, citing lack of evidence. Also among the accused were Kalyan Singh and Vinay Katiyar. It is unlikely that the BJP-led Uttar Pradesh government will take steps to appeal the judgement, as its own senior members were involved in the case. This is where it all ends, and no amount of criticism directed by the Opposition against the CBI or the UP government can perhaps reverse the verdict that will be passed down in history as the official story of the Babri Masjid demolition.

## THE HIPPOCRATIC OATH

'This is pure business ... don't think it is social service.'
                                        Dateline: 1 September 2017

The quote above articulates perfectly the philosophy of private healthcare providers across the country.

It is an open secret that private hospitals fleece their patients. This is enough for Umesh Patil, another gutsy investigative journalist working with Cobrapost, to take on the task of sieving through the various corrupt practices that private hospitals indulge in, often to the detriment of patients who trust them with their lives.

Donning the hat of a manager of a small, private nursing home, Patil goes about meeting the senior marketing staff of some of the major private hospitals, asking them what kind of commission they would offer for patient referrals. Patil has a close call while he is interviewing a senior manager of Jaslok Hospital. The manager becomes suspicious, and asks if he is recording the conversation. He even checks Patil's mobile. Fortunately, his mobile had discharged and got switched off.

When Patil wraps up his investigation, he has in his grasp twenty major hospitals with well-oiled patient referral systems in place to reward doctors or smaller hospitals for sending them patients for specialised treatment. Spread across Delhi-NCR, Bangalore and Bombay, these are super-specialty healthcare providers, many with multiple branches in a single city. The major findings of his investigation are that each hospital pays out a commission ranging between 10 and 30 per cent of the total bill, and the implications of such a practice—hospitals overcharge their patients to pay these commissions.

Procedures like a knee transplant could fetch a commission of Rs 25,000, while a liver transplant could fetch Rs 1.5 lakh. No surprise, then, if a patient is kept on a ventilator unnecessarily for days on end. There are also many other hidden charges. Such practices are forbidden under the Medical Council of India guidelines. But who cares about guidelines when every institution has become permissive?

We break the story on 1 September 2017. Asian Heart Hospital files a police complaint against Cobrapost. Ironically, the hospital had put up hoardings across Bombay a few months earlier, proclaiming 'No Commission to Doctors'.

Strangely, while it first agrees to run the story in full, Times Now stops broadcasting our findings after naming three hospitals. I am not surprised that the Medical Council of India does not take notice of the story. Maybe there are business interests to protect; the story exposes almost all the marquee names in healthcare: Fortis, JP Hospital, Metro Hospital, Yashoda Hospital, Columbia Asia Hospital, MAX Hospitals, Apollo Hospital, BLK Super Speciality Hospital, Nanavati Super Speciality Hospital, Hiranandani Hospital, Asian Heart Institute, Seven Hills Hospital, Jaslok Hospital, Narayana Hrudayalaya College of Nursing and Mallya Hospital.

## CATCH ME IF YOU CAN

Hizbul does another RTI-based story on 4 November 2017. 'Digging Deeper for Profits' shows how water bottling companies are squeezing dry the earth's groundwater, depleting the water table, and thus making life difficult for local communities. This open corporate looting of a most vital natural resource has gone on unabated for years, under license from the government.

It is not rare for reporters to face tricky situations when covering such anti-corruption stories. Like his senior colleagues Ashish and Syed, Hizbul faced a perilous situation during an assignment in Uttar Pradesh in 2016, some months before the assembly elections. Over the years, a trend has emerged of politicians asking for support in kind for their election campaigns. Pursuing some leads, Hizbul met leaders of various political parties to see if they engaged in this practice. The proposition was simple: we will provide you banners, posters and other campaign support, and in return, you will ensure us steady business for the next five years.

After speaking to some politicians, Hizbul went to meet a Samajwadi Party leader in Meerut. The meeting went smoothly, with the politician happily agreeing to look after the business interests of his prospective financial supporter. His son was also present. As the meeting was about to end, some other party functionaries trooped in. The leader asked his son to conclude the parley with Hizbul. Hizbul was about to wrap things up when the son got suspicious. He was frisked, and his cover was blown. There was a huge ruckus, with Hizbul being pushed around. He revealed who he was and asked the security guard of the Samajwadi Party leader, a sitting MLA, to call the police. The Samajwadi Party leader issued a statement saying Hizbul was a suspected terrorist, and the police and the media believed this while we worked overtime to establish his true identity. Fortunately, one of my colleagues, Sanjeev Yadav, knew the SHO personally. But Hizbul still had to spend twenty-four hours at the Delhi Gate police station.

## WHAT THE MEDIA WANTS TO HIDE FROM YOU

'I personally got a phone call from the PMO. They told us to give them data saying maybe some of the stone-pelters [in J&K] are Paytm users.'

Dateline: 26 March 2018

Over the years, newsrooms have become war rooms, and prime-time debates have turned into high-decibel duels as the media panders to a particular ideology, promoting a divisive agenda, whipping up communal hatred and publishing paid content masquerading as news. In these days of agenda-driven journalism, the sobriquet of 'godi media' is apt for the Indian version of embedded journalism.

Those who are in the business of news, in any manner, know how far and wide the phenomenon of paid news spreads.

Simply put, paid news is an attempt to build public opinion by disseminating information that may or may not be true. It denies the consumers of news access to correct information; its source is vitiated, and it is aimed at serving particular interests. Paid news compromises a viewer's right to freely exercise choice, particularly when it comes to casting votes, thus undermining the spirit and practice of democracy. Politicians of all hues use paid news to influence voters. Various institutions such as the Election Commission of India, the Parliamentary Standing Committee, the Law Commission and the Press Council of India have taken due cognisance of the issue of paid news, and have, from time to time, taken measures to stem the rot. However, in the absence of a strong political will, such efforts have been merely symbolic in their approach and effect. The Press Council of India's action to set up an inquiry committee in 2009 is a prime example. Rather than taking the bull by its horns, the media watchdog chose to bury the report compiled by senior journalists Paranjoy Guha-Thakurta and K. Srinivas Reddy, which nailed some of the biggest media groups in the country.

At some point, journalist Pushp Sharma comes to us with the many shoots he's already done on the issue. He needs support to go the whole distance. Initially, I have doubts about taking on my own fraternity, but somebody has to bell the cat. Cobrapost's Operation 136 brings the buried truth out into the full glare of national attention. Although the basic premise of the story can be defined as paid news, its ambit goes well beyond.

Sharma ends up doing some amazing work in the field for this story. He devises a simple plan. He poses as a pracharak from a fictitious religious organisation with loads of money and an agenda for influencing the 2019 Lok Sabha elections. Then he calls on various media organisations, and asks them to run his media campaign, the three main ingredients of which are:

- Promotion of Hindutva, disguised as spiritual discourse.
- Mobilisation of electorates on communal lines.
- Defamation of Opposition leaders by lampooning them.

In return, Sharma promises to channel them money in the form of advertisements, sometimes even cash.

Shockingly, almost all the media organisations, whether print, electronic or digital, agree to run this communal and defamatory campaign. We expose forty-eight media organisations, some of them leaders in the news industry, both mainstream and regional. There are hardly any marquee names missing from the list.

*Bartman* and *Dainik Samvad*, both regional newspapers, stand out among the lot for refusing to play ball.

Operation 136 is completely blacked out by the mainstream media. But the story is carried by alternative platforms, and gets a phenomenal response on social media. Some international media organisations, such as Al Jazeera, the BBC and the *Guardian*, cover the story.

It is clear that money can buy media organisations. We learn the following:

- These organisations are ready to promote Hindutva in the garb of spiritualism, publish content to polarise the electorate along communal lines and defame the political rivals of the party in power.
- They are willing to plant stories in favour of the party in power.
- Some of them are associated with the RSS or have pro-Hindutva leanings.
- Many are willing to accept cash for their services, with some even able to suggest ways in which black money can be routed through angadias to be delivered as white.

- They can defame any political leader, however highly placed, from any political party—whether in power or in the Opposition.

It is painful to watch members of these organisations genuflect before a supposedly big-ticket client.

Cobrapost becomes a media bad boy and loses a lot of friends after it breaks the story. Some of the organisations that we name have had commercial contracts for content with Cobrapost in the past. But the story is shortlisted for the Global Shining Light Award of the Global Investigative Journalism Network in 2019.

## THE DHFL SCAM

Sometime in late 2018, after receiving tip-offs about the non-banking financial company (NBFC) sector and in particular about Dewan Housing Corporation Limited (DHFL), we start investigating a new story. Solely from scrutinising public records, we find that the primary promoters of DHFL, Kapil and Dheeraj Wadhawan, have engineered a scam of close to Rs 31,000 crore. The scam was pulled off mainly by sanctioning and disbursing astronomical amounts in secured and unsecured loans to dubious shell or pass-through companies related to DHFL's own primary stakeholders, Kapil Wadhawan, Dheeraj Wadhawan and Aruna Wadhawan, through their proxies and associates. These entities, in turn, passed the money on to companies controlled by the Wadhawans. The money was then used to buy shares, equity and other private assets in India and abroad, including the UK, Dubai, Mauritius and Sri Lanka.

By lending to shell or pass-through companies without due diligence, DHFL ensured that the recovery of such dubious loans would be impossible, since the companies or their directors themselves did not own any assets. This way, the private assets acquired by the Wadhawans and their associates by using these dubious loans were completely ring-fenced from any recovery process that may be initiated by authorities under the SARFAESI Act or the Insolvency and Bankruptcy Code of India. Thus, the only losers in the process were the public sector banks, such as State Bank of India and Bank of Baroda, with an exposure of over Rs 11,000 crore and Rs 4,000 crore respectively, as well as foreign banks and shareholders from among the public, or investors, of DHFL.

What helped Kapil Wadhawan and Dheeraj Wadhawan pull off the scam was the position of power and influence they occupied as majority members in the finance committee of DHFL, which was responsible for approving loans of Rs 200 crore and above to any entity. Together, DHFL and its primary promoters created dozens of shell entities with a nominal capital of Rs 1 lakh, divided them into small groups of two to four companies, with a lot of them having the same or similar addresses with the same set of initial directors, and on many occasions having the same group of auditors to mask the financial details.

They also granted loans amounting to thousands of crores to these shell companies in the name of secured loans against slum development projects without any due diligence or maintaining an adequate debt–equity ratio. They had the gumption to disburse the loan in single tranches rather than following the established norm of disbursal in stages, against progress of the project works. Conscious of the fraud they were committing, they ensured that most of the shell companies hid the name of the lender, DHFL, the terms of loan and the terms of repayment in their financial statements. Using the loan money dubiously advanced by DHFL, these companies gave donations to several political parties. They created offshore assets of at least Rs 4,000 crore and did flashy stuff like buying Wayamba, a Sri Lankan Premier League cricket team.

Shockingly, no bank or auditing agency had thus far flagged any of these suspicious transactions. How could the RBI, and other lending banks or auditing firms, who had much greater access to financial documents than we did, have not seen or raised concerns over such gross irregularities? What had they been doing? It seemed all the regulatory bodies had been sleeping peacefully while crores of public money disappeared in broad daylight.

If the entire scam could be worked out by a bunch of journalists diligently scouring through public documents in a month or so, why hadn't the regulators and the banks who loaned DHFL the money shown similar focus?

We release the story by way of a press conference. Though we send more than five dozen question to DHFL, they aren't answered. Instead, the company makes a big hue and cry about not getting enough time to answer the questions.

Subsequently, the company 'recruits' a so-called 'independent auditor', Motilal Oswal Financial Services, to prove us wrong. Obviously, the tactic doesn't work. We reply with actual details of the transactions, and make all the papers public to debunk DHFL's 'independent' auditors. The fallout is huge. The government and the RBI immediately institute independent enquiries against the DHFL promoters. The Uttar Pradesh government joins the fray as more than Rs 2000 crore of its employees' provident fund money has been invested in DHFL, through the bribery of higher officials. All the statutory and regulatory bodies suddenly wake up and start investigating the financial irregularities of DHFL. And the worms are soon crawling out of the can. Eventually, it is proven that DHFL has colluded with a cousin of the Wadhawan brothers—Sarang

(Sunny) Wadhawan, the son of their uncle, Rakesh Wadhawan—in what is to become the infamous HDIL case that results in the bankruptcy of the Punjab Maharashtra Bank and the evaporation of hundreds of crores of taxpayers' money. Sunny Wadhawan is arrested, and during investigation, his links to the underworld don Iqbal Mirchi, as well as to the Wadhawan brothers, come to the fore.

Within a year, DHFL's shares fall from above Rs 390 to Rs 40. DHFL, with a debt of nearly Rs 98,200 crore, and it reports a loss of Rs 2,223 crore in the quarter ending 31 March 2019. Enquiries lead the Security and Exchanges Board of India to propose stricter disclosure norms for auditing agencies of listed companies, which is one of the best consequences of any investigation I have been involved in.

Soon, our investigations are vindicated by other independent agencies, and Deloitte Haskin and Sells LLP resign as internal auditors of DHFL. They submit a detailed report about the irregularities they have found in DHFL's financials, including several violations and inconsistencies. Despite citing Section 143(1) to access additional information from DHFL in the case of certain transactions, the auditors say that they have gained no satisfactory response from the company. Chaturvedi and Shah LLP, DHFL's other internal auditor, follow suit and resign as well, citing significant deficiencies in the grant and rollover of Rs 5,652 crore of inter-corporate deposits, and lack of sufficient information and explanations regarding credit, legal and technical evaluation and evidence for end-use monitoring of loans worth nearly Rs 24,000 crore. Our numbers stand validated by these auditors.

The worst isn't over for DHFL. In 2019, the Enforcement Directorate institutes an independent inquiry, which ultimately points at misappropriation of funds to the tune of Rs 25,000 crore by the promoters of DHFL in the alleged financial fraud. Earlier, after our story first broke, the directorate had suspected DHFL of diverting loans worth Rs 12,773 crore to seventy-nine 'shadowy' companies allegedly associated with its promoters Kapil Wadhawan and Dheeraj Wadhawan between 2010 and 2015, but the amount in question turns out to be much more.

It is important to point out that none of the big financial scams reported in India have ever been broken by 'business' or 'finance' publications or business channels. A cosy partnership has developed between corporates and the business media which has prohibited this. This is not to say that there aren't talented journalists working in these platforms. It's just this requirement for access to top management for day-to-day repertorial purposes mixed with commercial priorities that make deep-dive investigations a liability for media platforms.

# EPILOGUE

When I was about seventeen and living in Allahabad, a sanyasi showed up at our home near Bamrauli airport. He got food and tea and conversation from us and went on his way. This soon became a routine. Once a week, for maybe five years, he would come to our house, till my father got transferred to Calcutta in 1988.

The sanyasi stayed on the banks of the river Ganga, near an old settlement called Salim Sarai, halfway between the city of Allahabad and the airport. In a temple nearby stayed his old, blind guru, whom he used to take care of. Once a week, he would walk about ten kilometres to the market of Begum Sarai, where vegetable sellers would provide him vegetables free of cost. Our house was located about two kilometres from Begum Sarai, and he would stop for tea on his way, chat with us, and be off. He always wore a sweater, even in the summer months, and I would always pick on him for that. He would say that his sweater was his 'cooler'. That it made him sweat, and then, when the wind blew, he felt cool.

As I ruminate over the years that have passed, the sanyasi returns often to my mind. Once, I asked him what he did in his ashram by the river, and he said, '*Bus Ram naam ghistey rahtey hain.*' I just keep repeating the name of Ram.

I don't know whether he is still alive or not, but his rustic faith has always inspired me and made me nostalgic.

Passing time during this pandemic-induced lockdown has afforded me an opportunity to gaze at birds from my balcony, reflect on the close relationships I have had, and recollect the stories that my uncles told me of their growing-up years, as well as stories that leapt out of my own head, from strange recesses I had almost forgotten existed.

I remember Girish uncle narrating to me the story of when he was caught smoking at the age of six. I would not do justice to the story if I didn't reproduce his recollection of the event verbatim from a letter he wrote in 1981 to his cousin to console him on his father's (and Girish uncle's mama's) death.

> My memory goes back more than forty years to Unnao. I was then only six. Bhaiye did not smoke then but he kept a tin of cigarettes in the drawing room to offer to the visitors. I dearly wanted to try one of them. One day, when he had gone to the office and Mami was having a nap, I sneaked into the drawing room and took out a cigarette and attempted to light it. But instead of inhaling it, I exhaled the breath several times as one does while lighting a fire. The cigarette never lighted and I threw the unlit cigarette out of the window in disgust. Then I tried a second and a third. but nothing happened and this continued for days on end and the tin became emptier everyday till inevitably Bhaiye noticed it. Suspicion naturally fell on Kanhai, the servant. But before he could be questioned, Kanhai caught me red-handed in the act of trying to light a cigarette and promptly reported the matter to Bhaiye when he came home in order to save his good name. Bhaiye did not scold me nor did he lecture me about the evils of smoking. All he did was to ask Kanhai to get him the tin. He extracted a cigarette from the tin and said he would teach me how to smoke and then I could try one. He put the cigarette in between my lips,

lighted it and asked me to inhale. The next moment, the roof fell on me. My throat choked and I realised what a foul thing it was. He then made me write a letter to my mother saying that I had smoked a cigarette and that I would never do it again. And I never did, for almost twenty years. I had learnt a lesson by a single puff which I might not have, by scolding or sermons.

From cigarettes my memories take me to Iraq.

I remember being held up for thirty minutes at a militia checkpoint in Najaf, in 2004, because when they searched my backpack they found an Indian notebook, which had the face of Karishma Kapoor on the back. How could I be in the possession of a notebook with a beautiful girl's picture? The guards were part of the retinue of Grand Ayotallah Sistani, whom I was trying to interview for a story for *Outlook* magazine. They also guarded the holy Shia shrine in Najaf. Being an Indian 'sahafi' or writer helped me, but only after I answered dozens of questions. Eventually, they tore up the last page of the notebook and let me through.

I have many more memories of Najaf. At that time, there were about a dozen students from India, studying religion under various ayotallahs. The climate was unbearably hot, and their living conditions were medieval. I felt I had to contribute towards an air conditioner for them in their study hall so that they could at least study in peace. The students wouldn't accept this contribution, as they first wanted permission from their ayotallah, who happened to be a Shia of Pakistani origin, perhaps in his seventies. The ayotallah looked at me with a very puzzled expression when I went to his seminary to ask his permission to buy the air conditioner. 'Sure, it won't be a problem,' he said in Arabic. The students translated for me. Though I spoke to him in Urdu, he chose to only reply in Arabic. Throughout our conversation, I could see his gaze returning time and again to the assortment of Hindu temple threads on my wrist. When he could no longer contain the question, he asked me why I was helping Muslim students though I was a Hindu.

I told him that it didn't matter to me whether they were Muslims or Hindus. They were students from India and far away from home. I just wanted to do my bit.

The pandemic has opened doors to memories of books that I prized growing up. In my teens, I was a big fan of Western novels, especially the Sudden series by Oliver Strange and Frederik H. Christian. I have now bought the books, and am busy savouring them all over again.

Sudden, the protagonist of the series—which Strange started off in the 1930s with *The Range Robbers*—is an outlaw turned undercover law officer. The fastest gunman in the West, Sudden goes off to look for enemies of his foster father, and ends up solving other messes along the way. It is an electric moment in every book when he announces, usually in a salon, 'My name is Jim Green. They also call me Sudden.' Those words are enough to cause everyone there to freeze!

My own moment of freezing happened in a conversation with Naipaul sometime in 2002. On one of his visits to India, he and Lady Nadira took me out to dinner. There, he grilled me for about two hours on the kind of books I read, my socio-economic condition and, more specifically, whether I had a peaceful atmosphere at home, in which to write steadily. I remember we spoke of Ryszard Kapuscinski and a host of other travel writers. He gave me a lot of advice that night about what to read to become a better writer. 'You have to read a lot of history,' he said. 'Without being rooted in a historical context, your writing will be ill-informed.'

Then he proceeded to educate me about the different periods of world history I should delve into for inspiration. Within a few months, I had ordered about a hundred books on world history, but I specifically took to ancient Greek history. It was a world that fascinated and inspired me so much that I imagined a historical novel in those settings. I wrote *The Emissary* a few years later, and it got published by Fourth Estate in 2010. Set in the times of Alexander the Great, it traces the life of Seleucus, son of Nicanor. While I was writing the novel, my daughters were still young and would peer at my laptop screen over my shoulders, wondering what exactly it was that I was doing. My elder one once spilled her milk over my laptop. Purposely, I think, as she felt that she wasn't getting enough attention from me! She still remembers the rollicking she got. She turned out to be the biggest fan of the book, and hectors me to write a sequel.

There is a funny memory related to *Bunker 13* that keeps coming back to me every now and then. In 2003, when I was in Barcelona, promoting the launch of the Spanish edition of the book, my publishers placed a Gillette shaving razor, a shaving foam canister and a massage oil bottle alongside every copy of the book for the journalists coming for the reading. I didn't get it at first. I thought the gimmick was some bit of Spanish media culture, where gifts like razors flew. Then I read the press release, which reproduced certain passages from the novel, and mentioned the page numbers they corresponded to. As understanding dawned, I nearly choked with laughter. I reproduce one para below, so you get the drift of it:

> Shaving pubic hair is an art in itself. The skill lies in making it an enjoyable experience for the woman. You ease Sally's stiffness and apprehension by spraying on her a liberal dose of foam. Then you start rubbing the foam on her mound till she stops giggling. That's when you know that she has entered the pleasure zone. You have to allow ten minutes for the foam to soften the hair roots. Most shavers don't have the patience to work this time into their schedule and that makes the razor work tough.

The pandemic is making me assess how to live the balance of my years on the planet. I am getting back to fiction, my first love. I am working on a novel set in Europe, and also giving final shape to a novel set in Iraq in the insurgency years, after the American invasion of the country in 2003.

I guess journalism will always be there, but India today is hardly a place where you can be confident of judicial protection after doing a story that exposes corruption and hurts politicians and political parties. Till about half a decade back, you could make a reasonable assumption that the judiciary, though overworked and slow, held on to some basic fundamentals which wouldn't let it veer off its historical moorings. However, increasingly, the courts aren't as fastidious in protecting activists, journalists, RTI practitioners and whistleblowers from the egregious prosecutions of a state that has become unhinged.

Freedom of expression has become a casualty at all levels. A chill factor and self-censorship are increasingly evident in all media platforms. In the middle of all this, there are those who have allowed their platforms and themselves to be used as propaganda instruments for the state. They see no merit in a pluralistic society and drum up imaginary threats against the majority. They look at ways and means to spin the narrative in a way that could aid the state or a particular ideology. The steady encroachment on the rights of citizens has been supported by the mainstreaming of an ideology that doesn't feel it has to push back against lynchings, rioting, and the disenfranchisement of the country's minorities.

Journalists from different media platforms often contact me, complaining about how they can get absolutely nothing that is remotely critical of the establishment to fly past their editors. This is an ugly India in the making.

In 2002, at the peak of the NDA regime's hostility against *Tehelka* and its journalists, I applied for an arms license, and former home minister L.K. Advani himself intervened and saw to it that I got a non-civilian bore license out of turn. There is no way that journalists under threat would receive the same treatment from the government now.

I may be the only civilian in India's history to have been given a non-prohibited bore license apart from sportspersons, and this was possible primarily because the democratic veneer had still not totally vanished from the politicians governing us in those days. When I did meet the BJP leadership socially, they were always cordial and had long chats with me. I remember a two-hour chat with Arun Jaitley over players in the Indian cricket team. This was in 2003, before the UPA came to power and at the height of the NDA's vendetta against us. He badgered me about breaking the *Tehelka* story on 13 March 2001, the day V.V.S. Laxman scored his historic 281 at Eden Gardens against Australia. '*Koi aur din chun lete,*' he said mischievously. You could have chosen some other day.

I don't see that conviviality in today's leadership. I don't want to be misunderstood. I was under no illusion that Jaitley was a friend, but at least he could hold an interesting conversation. Vajpayee's government was in many ways more vengeful and perhaps had a smoother way of doing things. However, you could always argue that they had a certain sophistication rather than the crass way of bludgeoning dissent that dominates currently.

Of course, I never did buy a .38 because of the cost involved and the fact that, with the import of guns being prohibited since the V.P. Singh era, there is no way of knowing the history of a weapon. In those days, I was getting many threats. And no theoretical, journalistic principle was going to stop me from defending my young family.

My kids have graduated now. They ask me questions about my early years. Though it's just a small window to what life has been like for me, this book will answer some of them.

I would like to leave you with one more memory, a recurring one for me. Every three months or so, I wake up in the middle of the night, dreaming that the next day is my physics examination. When I wake up, a wave of relief passes through me at the realisation that I am already a graduate and that there is no physics exam lurking around the corner!

As long as there is no physics involved, life can keep coming at me. I'll be ready.

# ACKNOWLEDGEMENTS

My eternal love for the late Sham Sawroop Bakshi, Dwarkanath guruji, Dada, Madan-ji, Lakshmi and Monu. For Devi Das Gurukal, Satish-ji, Sarvanan, Unnikrishnan, Ganapathi Namboodri, the Kathamadam family, Jayakrishnan, Radhakrishnan, the Vasudev family, Neelu and Sanket Maharaj, Niladri Maharaj, Somnath Maharaj, Ram Sevak, Girish and Raghunath Bhat, Kalidasa Bhat, Cielo Osorio, Chema and Yaina Kamejeia.

My uncles and aunts: Girish and Kamla, Uma, Kailash and Sashi, and Deepak. And Seema, Rajendra, Dilip, Ashok. My brothers and sisters: Raju bhaiya, Sunita didi, Neil Mehra, Dipali didi, Madhav Mehra, Mahim Mehra, Deepa bhabhi, Ashish Mehra, Praveen and Bharti, Vinay and Nandini, Chayan Mehra, Asit Mehra, Divya, Disha, Gopal Bahal, Satish Bahal, Pankaj Bahal, Sanjay Bahal, Neelu, Harsha Bahal, Gaurav Tandon, and our late Vijay bhaiya.

Our lawyers, for always being there with their advice and time, and for being more friends than lawyers:

Prashant Bhushan, who is in a league of one. Pramod Dubey, Sidhartha Agarwal, Raj Shekhar Rao, Satyanarain Vashishth, Ruby Ahuja, Medhanshu Tripathi, Amit Prasad, Rishad Medora,

Shri Singh, Kotla Harshavardhana, Amit Agarwal, Pritha Srikumar, K.B. Nalwa, Satyajit Sarna, Karan Joseph, Aniketh Chandrashekhar, Mansi Sood, Pallavi Srivastava, Nishank Matoo, Shiv Chopra, Anchal Tikmani, Hemant Shah, Anand Venkatramani, Rishab Jain and Veresh Saharya.

And the seniors who have always helped: Kapil Sibal, Rajiv Dhawan, Dushyant Dave, Raju Ramachandran, Gopal Subramanium, Arvind Nigam, Siddhartha Luthra, Mahesh Agarwal, Meet Malhotra, Siddharth Dave, Kevin Gulati, Akshay Bhan and Nikhil Nayyar.

My friends, who have supported my endeavours over the last decade, and not in any particular order: the late Gillon Aitken, Shankar and Devina Sharma, T.N.V. Iyer, Vibhav Kant Upadhyaya, Raghav Bahl, Uday Shankar, the late Indrajit Bannerjee, Mahua Moitra, Pavan Khera, Ketaki, the late Somesh Mehrotra, Danny Gaekwad, Karthika V.K., Vikrant Jindal, Ravi Mohan Sethi, Ashish Kumar, Anil Kapoor, Milind Deora, Rifat Jawaid, Monica Mirza, Shailja, Shikha Pandey, Sadhna, Anurag Sehgal, Sanjay Salil, Siddharth Vardarajan, Yashwant Deshmukh, Manav Singh, Nooraine Fazal, Gargi Bhattacharya, Usha Ramanathan, Dr Ajay Shah, Rashi Mehra, Ashish Porwal, Ambrish and Ruchi, Shekhar Bhatia, Nachi, Tanuj Pandey, Ram Sapkota, Vinu, George Varghese, Sandeep Yash, Suhasini, Piyush Jain, Amit Goel, Biswadeep Moitra, Ashutosh, Shivam Vij, Anoop Gupta, Vineet Narain, Rajesh Kalra, Monica Halan, Govind Ethiraj, Nitin Khanna, Deepak Sharma, Nirupama Sekhri, Abhinandan, Meenakshi, Ajit Sahi, Krishna Prasad, Nilou Ahmadzadeh, Swamy, Rituparna Chatterjee, Pankaj Pachauri, Naveen and Shalu Jindal, Ranjan-ji, Arvind Arya, Mahesh Donia, Rahul Pathak, Ashish Khetan, Rajdeep and Sagarika, Rajeev Mehrotra, Subi Chaturvedi, Harpal Singh, Dalip Singh, Suresh, Abhisar Sharma, Kavita Mallick, Vikram Singh, Manoj Mitta, Pranjoy Guha Thakurta, Satyashree Gandham, Sandhya

Ravishankar, Vivian Fernandes, Josy Joseph, Manu Joseph, Karan Boolani, Tighmanshu Dhulia, Ravi Chandra, Hartosh Singh Bal, Ashish Chopra, Vinod Jose, Rishadat Kabeer, Anuj Srivastava, Kumar Baadal, Emma Toducz, Ushinor Mazumdar, Fayaz Rizvi, Sharad Vyas, Satish Singh, Shahzeb Khan, Sumit Joshi, Karan Talwar, Bhanu, Anuranjan Jha, Commodore Lokesh Batra, Sunil Khosla, Nirmal Bansal, Atul Mehra, Adriana Marcela, Shaqueel, Smanto, Niraj Kumar, Shahzeb, Guha and Mekala.

My Cobrapost family, present and former. Special thanks to Rakesh, Praval, Raju, Rajesh, Deepak, Ajay, Laksmi, Rohit and Pankaj.

My Skopje friends: Aleksej Aleksik, Milivoje Gjorgjevikj, Marjan Nakov, Anastasija, Jordance Illiev, Martin Laveresky.

My parents Kedar and Meena, Suresh Bakshi, Savita and Hemant, and my daughters Rhea and Esha, for being supportive of my madness.

www.ingramcontent.com/pod-product-compliance
Lightning Source LLC
LaVergne TN
LVHW010313070526
838199LV00065B/5547